C000129180

AC/DC

THE STORY OF THE ORIGINAL MONSTERS OF ROCK

RIGHT: Bon gives Angus a lift in Hollywood, February 1977. The on-stage electricity between Bon Scott and Angus Young was key to the early success of AC/DC. Both were showmen who were loved by the crowds.

THIS IS A CARLTON BOOK

Published in Great Britain in 2015 by
Carlton Books Limited
20 Mortimer Street
London W1T 3JW

Previously published as *Treasures of AC/DC* in 2012

A CIP catalogue for this book is available from the British Library.

ISBN 978-1-78097-616-7

Printed in China

10 9 8 7 6 5 4 3 2 1

AC/DC

THE STORY OF THE ORIGINAL MONSTERS OF ROCK

Jerry Ewing

CARLTON
BOOKS

Contents

Introduction

AC/DC were the first band I ever got into. As a schoolboy growing up in Sydney in the 1970s they were unavoidable. I remember seeing them on television performing 'High Voltage' on some family entertainment show, the name of which escapes me. It wasn't *Countdown*, our only viable music outlet on television, because the whole family were sat there and I recall my mother commenting on how she liked the fact the guitarist was dressed as a schoolboy. I couldn't tell you what we'd had for tea that night, and I certainly can't remember what I was being taught at school at the time either, but I can remember seeing AC/DC on television and I remember what my mother, God rest her soul, said to me at the time.

That's the kind of impact the band have on their fans, and why I'm writing these words now. AC/DC speak a universal language, as indeed I happily discovered when we arrived here in England. Whether it's the leering but friendly grin of the late Bon Scott or the howay-the-lads character of Brian Johnson, be it Angus Young's implausibly intense fingers flying maniacally over his fretboard, the relentless rhythms churned out by older brother Malcolm or the frighteningly rock-steady beat of Cliff Williams and Phil Rudd, the music of AC/DC transcends boundaries, colours and creeds. If you don't get it, then you must be deaf. Or dead!

So I hope you enjoy this book and the treasures contained herein. AC/DC remain my favourite band, despite the myriad forms of music I've gotten into since that first encounter. And I enjoy them just as much today as I did back then. It's because they speak my language. And, obviously, they speak yours too.

"We want to appeal to everyone and get rich quick. We want to be millionaires. I've got this plan to buy Tasmania, you see..." *Angus*

LEFT: A very early AC/DC line-up, featuring (left to right) Rob Bailey, Angus Young, Malcolm Young, Dave Evans and Pete Clack.

Early Years

BELOW LEFT: The first AC/DC producers, George Young and Harry Vanda, in their Easybeats days. The band was together between 1964 and 1969.

BELOW: Angus (left) watches on as brothers Malcolm and George hammer out the band's latest rocker on the piano.

There are three factors in the make-up of AC/DC that simply cannot be denied: Glasgow, Sydney and family. They are the bedrock underpinning the ideals, mentality, work ethic and the very existence of the five piece rock 'n' roll band formed with such youthful enthusiasm in Sydney in November 1973. And much like their music, these ideals have never changed. This continuity has done a lot to make AC/DC the band they are, remaining true to themselves and giving scant regard to anything or anyone in their way.

The Young family was large: six brothers, Steven, John, Alex, George, Malcolm and Angus, and solitary sister Margaret, born to William and Margaret Young in the Cranhill area of Glasgow between 1933 and 1955. All would play their part in the eventual birth of AC/DC. William worked variously as a spray painter, Royal Air Force mechanic and a valve grinder, but by the 1950s Cranhill, a shipbuilding area, was experiencing something of an economic and social upheaval. With the government using the area to rehouse residents of previous inner-city dwellings, life on the streets was rough and tough, instilling in the Youngs a strong family ethic as a means of survival. This was a lesson well learned by AC/DC guitarists Malcolm and Angus Young.

Besides playing typical kids' games on Cranhill's streets, hard-up families looked to themselves for entertainment. The Youngs' chosen form of recreation was a family band featuring brothers Steve, John and Alex on accordion and guitars. Alex would eventually pursue his own musical goals, moving to Germany to play saxophone with Tony Sheridan (with whom The Beatles had once played): but back in the early 1960s such success wasn't even a distant dream. William Young was finding it tough to support such a large family, and decided to take advantage of the Australian government's assisted passage offer; in 1963 the remaining members of the Young clan became "£10 Poms", as British migrants were referred to in Australia, when they were uprooted and transplanted to Sydney.

It was a journey similar to that taken seven years earlier by another Scottish family, Chick and Isa Scott and their children Graeme, Valerie and young Ronald Belford, nicknamed Bon, who had moved from Kirriemuir to Melbourne before settling in Perth.

George Young wasted little time in pursuing his own musical dreams and formed a band in Villawood, the area of Sydney where the Youngs' migrant hostel was situated. Called The Easybeats, their brand of beat pop, inspired by the music being created back in the UK, earned them a deal with new Sydney record label Albert Productions. Owner Ted Albert took them under his wing, and by 1965 The Easybeats had hit number 1 in Australia with 'She's So Fine'. A year later came an international hit with 'Friday On My Mind', and they took off for England.

Deprived of the company of their closest older brother, Malcolm and young Angus bonded tightly. They didn't fare well at Ashfield Boys' High School; George, not academic success, was their inspiration. Mother Margaret bought them their first guitars, despite William disapproving of more of his clan choosing music as a career. When The Easybeats' Harry Vanda gave Malcolm his 1963 Gretsch Firebird because he didn't like its tone, and Malcolm handed down his Hofner to Angus, their destiny seemed certain.

Angus had been taken to see Louis Armstrong by his sister Margaret and been deeply impressed. Like Malcolm, he devoured new musical sounds such as John Mayall's Bluesbreakers,

Hendrix and Cactus. They went to see the likes of The Yardbirds, The Who and The Small Faces. By the time they left school, Malcolm in 1967 and Angus two years later, there was only one thing the brothers wanted.

Malcolm performed with a succession of local bands with names such as Beelzebub Blues and Rubberband before The Easybeats' singer Stevie Wright put him in touch with another Sydney band called The Velvet Underground, whose touring schedule took him out of the city for the first time. Angus, meanwhile, was training as a printer, but saved enough to buy his first Gibson SG (as used by his then-heroes Pete Townshend and Mountain's Leslie West). Soon he'd formed Kantuckee (later Tantrum), who performed in Sydney clubs such as Chequers, Angus often claiming he was a dwarf to explain his small stature and under age. One night he tripped over his guitar lead; determined not to be left shamefaced, he continued flailing around the floor, all the while wringing torturous sounds from his SG. His signature stage style was born.

Having seen Led Zeppelin, The Rolling Stones and Muddy Waters in Sydney in 1972 and 1973, Malcolm decided to form his own band. Angus had just left Tantrum and Malcolm invited him to join his new outfit. As they pondered a name, sister Margaret suggested AC/DC, having seen it on her sewing machine.

Meanwhile in Perth, Bon Scott had been making musical inroads of his own.

BELOW: Malcolm Young hard at it in the studio while Angus takes a cigarette break.

The 1970s

The early years of AC/DC were both their busiest and, for a band such as this, their most exciting: five working-class youths railing against the ills they perceived in society and striking out on their own, discovering a world in tune with their ideals and lifestyle, a world that would extend beyond their native Australia and eventually take in the rest of the planet, and which brought with it the rewards appropriate to rock superstardom.

It was also a hard slog: but then, AC/DC set out with the right work ethic and mindset. The world was theirs for the taking, and they were damn sure they were going to give it their best shot, or at least go down fighting in a blaze of glory.

Malcolm Young's original line-up also included brother Angus, vocalist Dave Evans, bassist Larry Van Kriedt and drummer Colin Burgess. They played their very first gig at Sydney's now legendary Chequers venue on December 31, 1973. The band were deemed too loud by management, but Chequers' entertainment manager Gene Pierson was struck by something about the band and booked them into the equally legendary (in the AC/DC story at least) Bondi Lifesavers' Club, where they began to build a solid and loyal following.

The original line-up lasted a mere four months and changed frequently, sometimes several times a month in the early days, as the driven Malcolm Young sought the right ingredients. Pierson remained influential in the band's early development; it was his friendship with Ted Albert that allowed the band to secure a deal with the Albert label, with which the band – then consisting of Malcolm, Angus, Evans, bassist Rob Bailey and drummer Pete Clack – recorded the single 'Can I Sit Next To You Girl'. However, the band remained unhappy with Evans, who was strongly influenced by glam rock, and Pierson was instrumental in his replacement by the band's roadie, Bon Scott.

With Scott in place, things moved on apace. They began work in earnest on their debut album for Albert, *High Voltage*, which featured a re-recorded version of the band's debut single. The easygoing Scott's natural bonhomie and broader view of the world than the other band members, not to mention his primal howl, helped keep the band's army of fans growing.

High Voltage made inroads for the band in Australia, as did the follow-up, 1975's *T.N.T.*, by which time the line-up had solidified: Young, Young, Scott, bassist Mark Evans and drummer Phil Rudd. The band's knack for penning anthemic songs that struck a chord with Australia's fast-growing legion of rock-loving youth helped drive them towards the top in their native land; 'It's A Long Way To The Top' was a prime example, as was 'High Voltage', and the band became regulars on Australia's major music TV show *Countdown*.

By 1976 the band had secured a worldwide deal with Atlantic Records, who recognized them as something above and beyond the run-of-the-mill Australian rock band, such as Skyhooks and

Sherbet, whose appeal never really crossed over to international audiences. An international compilation of the band's first two albums, named *High Voltage* in a nod to the band's electric moniker, was released in 1976, followed later in the year by *Dirty Deeds Done Dirt Cheap*.

AC/DC now made their first foray into Europe, relocating to the UK, appearing on *Sounds* magazine's now-legendary Lock Up Your Daughters tour and supporting the likes of Rainbow in Europe. Life was now a steady diet of touring and squeezing in as much writing and preparation for forthcoming records as they could. The band returned to Sydney to record *Let There Be Rock*, but soon after fired Evans, replacing him with British-born bassist Cliff Williams, leaving Rudd the only Australian-born member of the band.

On the back of the new album they ventured to America for the first time, supporting the likes of REO Speedwagon, Kiss, Rush, Styx and Cheap Trick, while continuing to make serious dents in the UK market. In 1978 came *Powerage*, their hardest-sounding album to date and perhaps a direct reaction to the rigours of life on the road, but Atlantic was concerned that 'Rock 'n' roll Damnation' hadn't been a hit and when it came to recording a follow-up, the band were pushed to break with long-time producers Vanda and Young and look elsewhere. They ultimately ended up with Mutt Lange, and the resulting album *Highway To Hell* proved to be the key to unlocking the treasures they'd worked so hard for throughout the preceding six years.

AC/DC were coming towards the end of their lengthy *Highway To Hell* tour when they discovered that the album had sold over more than a million in America. The door was finally open.

LEFT: Angus about to drop his shorts at a surprise gig at Sydney's Strata Hotel.

OPPOSITE: 'Jailbreak' photo shoot, which took place in Sydney's Lavender Bay. The road crew dressed as cops…

High Voltage

The first AC/DC album was released on February 17, 1975, although the title was reused for a later album that became their first internationally recognized LP.

The original *High Voltage* was released on the Albert label in Australia only and serves as a fairly good guide to what this bunch of lovable larrikins were all about sonically. Much like the embryonic AC/DC themselves, *High Voltage* is rough-hewn, ragged, yet crackling with youthful energy and verve.

The album was recorded in a mere ten days (or in fact nights, to keep costs down, a regular occurrence with young bands) during November 1974 at Albert's Sydney studios. George Young handled production duties with Easybeats bandmate Harry Vanda, a partnership continued on AC/DC's next five studio albums.

Given the fledgling AC/DC's fluctuating line-up, the fact that a range of personnel played on *High Voltage* might help explain its slightly disjointed feel when placed alongside the more assured sequencing of later albums such as *Let There Be Rock* or *Powerage*. Naturally the newly formed engine-room of Malcolm and Angus Young drove the album's sound; their drive and ambition burn through the nine tracks. Bon Scott had only been with the band for two months since replacing original singer Dave Evans, but it's a mark of the man that he already sounds as if he's fronted AC/DC for ever.

Much of this has to do with Scott's wordplay, a key ingredient of the band's appeal since he joined and his enduring posthumous legacy. On *High Voltage* he hits immediate high points with the salacious 'Little Lover', 'Love Song' and the rollicking 'She's Got Balls'. 'Little Lover' was developed from a song Malcolm penned when he was only 14, to which Scott added his ambiguous lyrics. 'Love Song' was originally known as 'Fell In Love', and was written by Malcolm and Dave Evans. Scott added new lyrics and

High Voltage

(Australian) Baby Please Don't Go/She's Got Balls/ Little Lover/Stick Around/Soul Stripper/You Ain't Got A Hold On Me/ Love Song/Show Business/ (International) It's A Long Way To The Top (If You Want To Rock 'n' Roll)/Rock 'n' Roll Sinner/The Jack/Live Wire/T.N.T./Can I Sit Next To You Girl/ Little Lover/She's Got Balls/High Voltage

it became the first single from the album, while the forceful 'She's Got Balls', probably *High Voltage*'s standout track, was Bon's ode to his ex-wife Irene.

Another notable track was a driving cover of Big Joe Williams' song 'Baby, Please Don't Go', popularized in the 1960s by Van Morrison's band Them. Though only the B-side of the 'Little Lover' single, it succeeded in attracting both attention and airplay, while 'Soul Stripper', penned by Malcolm and Angus Young alone, proved the potential of the youthful but determined brothers.

Despite arriving at the height of the glam rock craze, *High Voltage* clearly draws its inspiration from an earlier time. There are elements of melody and an ability with a backing chorus that suggest glam had not gone unnoticed by the young band, but there's also a strong hint of Free's bluesy hard rock and the chugging early rock 'n' roll sound of Chuck Berry, a sound that would swiftly develop into the band's trademark.

"I like to get in front of a crowd and rip it up."
Angus

ABOVE Rare Portuguese single with unique imagery. A classic rock illustration style.

Aside from the Young/Young/Scott axis, George Young helped out on bass and drum duties for the recording sessions (he sometimes stood in on bass at early AC/DC concerts). Also taking a turn behind the kit were Peter Clack, AC/DC's regular drummer at the time of recording, plus Tony Currenti and John Proud, both on the roster during 1974, while Rob Bailey featured on bass.

While the original *High Voltage* came housed in a red sleeve which depicted a small dog urinating on an electrical substation (a move which sent early shockwaves around Australia's notoriously conservative press) the sleeve for the international release was substantially different. In fact, the album had two covers: one for the American market, featuring an illustration of Angus used for the Australian single release 'It's A Long Way To The Top (If You Want To Rock 'n' Roll)', and another for Europe, depicting Bon and Angus. In subsequent years the US version has predominated.

When the band secured their international record deal with Atlantic, the label decided to take the best songs from the band's two Australia-only releases and combine them on an album introducing the band to a global market. Despite taking its name from the band's debut, only 'She's Got Balls' and 'Little Lover' made the international version. This meant that for many years, before the coming of the internet, the songs from the original *High Voltage* remained out of reach of fans unprepared to fork out vast sums for rare import copies. Some eventually appeared in 1984 on the North American and Japanese EP release *'74 Jailbreak*, and the remainder surfaced on the 2009 collection *Backtracks*.

BELOW: Angus – in nothing but underpants – about to leap from the speaker stack as Bon Scott looks on.

"It's nothing to do with us at all. Our success is down to the taste of the public." *Bon*

RIGHT: The band stylishly attired for their 1975 promotional shoot for the *High Voltage* album.

15

"It's just rock 'n' roll. A lot of the time we get criticized for it." *Angus*

> ## "I've never had a message for anyone in my entire life. Except maybe my room number."
>
> *Bon*

When the 'Delta Queen' touched eleven knots at full steam, a man needed something to steady his nerves.

In 1870, two Mississippi riverboats took part in a race from New Orleans to St. Louis.

The victorious sternwheeler completed the 1,200 miles in the record breaking time of three days, eighteen hours and thirty minutes—an average speed of just over 11 knots.

During the trip the passengers (to take their minds off such reckless speeds) amused themselves in various ways.

They gambled in the great gilt and plush casinos: a man could board the boat a millionaire in New Orleans and be thrown off penniless four days later in St. Louis.

And they refreshed themselves from time to time with the odd glass of Southern Comfort, with ice and soda.

In fact, it was for such sophisticated occasions that Southern Comfort had been invented.

A New Orleans man was responsible: shortly after the South had lost the Civil War, he devised a drink so original that the recipe ran to more than 100 pages.

It was the essence of smoothness. It had a rich amber glow, and a flavour of quite indescribable subtlety. Yet it had a strength and a warmth to it that could calm even the faintest heart as the Mississippi landscape rushed past at that breakneck 11 knots.

Turn on to High Voltage the electrifying album from AC/DC

K50257

'O' Band

Very few English Bands these days seem to be able to distill the best of English and American rock into a sound that they can truthfully call their own. Many have tried and failed, most don't even try, but 'O' have tried and, at last, succeeded.

Those of you with a memory for distinctive names and an eye for peculiar album sleeves will no doubt remember 'O' from their days at Epic Records, for whom they made two satisfactory but, let's be honest, un-sensational albums. Their potential was quite apparent however, and it became obvious that a scintillated, rejuvenated O would be capable of far greater things. Their snap act is now a lesson in aural and visual dynamics, their songs are much stronger and more memorable than they were, and the new album, WITHIN REACH—their first for United Artists, is almost unrecognisable from previous recordings.

So who are they, these maestros about to take the country by storm? Well the line-up reads:

Pix—Lead vocals and guitars
Craig Anders—Vocals, electric slide and pedal steel guitars
Jeff Bannister—Vocals, piano, fender rhodes organ and Synthesisers
Mark Anders—Bass guitar
Derek Ballard—Drums and percussion

AC/DC

Five clean cut young boys residing and working in Australia. Pure as the driven snow, playing music sweet to the ear—if you believe that, you'll believe anything!

There're five of them all right, and they've got more cheek than Ned Kelly!... and when it comes to playing rock 'n' roll... they play it loud... they play it tight... and they don't compromise!

Angus Young
Born: Glasgow—Scotland. Age: 16
Lead guitarist and schoolboy—younger brother of producer George Young, Angus has been known during a performance to cover five miles, roll around the stage, mount the speaker boxes, play with his teeth, play one handed, leap into the audience and back onto the stage in a single bound, and appear as SUPER ANGUS.

Some attribute his energy to his staple diet which consists of chocolate bars, chocolate milkshakes and Smarties, but Angus will tell you that it all started at the ripe old age of fourteen when he tripped over a guitar lead and fell on his back—he decided to make it look intentional and rolled around on the floor. It was the first time he received a standing ovation. From that day on he became a mover. His ambition: mainly to reach seventeen—he wouldn't mind a yacht one day so that he could wear a sailor's suit and captain's hat and get the girls like Hugh Hefner does.

He is part of AC/DC's songwriting team together with Malcolm and Bon, and is described by critics as a... bid leaving guitar player.

He also does a great impression of James Cagney!

Bon Scott
Born: Kirriemuir—Scotland. Age: 24
Vocalist and chaperone for AC/DC. Bon is the oldie of the band so naturally the boys look to him for sound advice when it comes to all the things that confront a young, touring rock 'n' roll band. The do's and dont's, such as avoiding the mayor's daughter.

He is hailed by critics as being one of the best rock's lyricists, and has the voice to match. Bon is a rough diamond, but under those tattoos and leather clothes beats a heart of gold... that ain't all...

Malcolm Young
Born: Glasgow—Scotland. Age: 20
Rhythm guitarist and second younger brother to George Young, Malcolm creates the foundation of the rocking music that is AC/DC. Not only is he a great guitarist and songwriter, but also a person with vision—he is the planner in AC/DC. He is also the quiet one, deep and extremely aware. This coupled with his good looks, makes him an extremely popular member of AC/DC.

Phillip Rudd
Born: Melbourne—Australia. Age: 21
Drummer and bodyguard to Angus. When Philip auditioned for the position with AC/DC he walked in and virtually took over. Just the sort of aggressive little rocker the boys were looking for.

The proof of his rapport with the other boys is on record. None of your fancy stuff, just gear rock 'n' roll drumming. His good looks and muscular build make him a perfect band member.

Mark Evans
Born: Melbourne—Australia. Age: 19
Good bass players are hard to find. There was no exception to the rule with AC/DC. Mark fell into the position at the bottom of the stairs of a Melbourne club (5 while being ejected by bouncers for some boyish prank. He recognised AC/DC about to enter the club, and mentioned that he was a bass player—an audition was immediately arranged, and he proved to be just what the boys were looking for... aggressive, funky, a good looker, and an excellent player. A perfect member to complete the line-up that is AC/DC.

They're not the kind of band to take home to meet Mother, in fact, there are plenty of parents who won't allow their kids to even bring AC/DC's records in the house.

That doesn't deter Angus, Malcolm, Bon, Mark and Phil—they only want to lay their music on people who want honest, loud and unADULTerated rock 'n' roll!

LEFT: AC/DC caught live in 1975 in Sydney's Victoria Park. Angus already has his trademark Gibson SG.

RIGHT: AC/DC played the 1976 Reading Festival. This programme is a great example of the contemporary design style.

T.N.T.

Released less than a year apart, AC/DC's first two albums could hardly be more different. Where *High Voltage* sounded like a band taking their first, albeit electrifying, steps into the wide world of rock 'n' roll, its follow-up sent the message that these guys weren't only in it for the long haul but just might have what's required to go all the way to the top.

True, the band had moved on rapidly, enjoying more live success and honing their overall sound, and created their own studio album. George Young and Harry Vanda, who had brought such class and experience to the production of *High Voltage*, were back on board: but this doesn't explain the transformation.

What marks *T.N.T.* out as the birth of the relentless AC/DC boogie machine is that it was recorded with a stable line-up, and one that would be in place for the next two years. Given that AC/DC had seen 18 line-up changes in as many months, (admittedly, mostly centred around the core trio of Malcolm, Angus and Bon), the simple fact that they'd stabilized their roster with new drummer Phil Rudd and bass player Mark Evans meant they could now concentrate on developing and polishing their unique, electrifying sound.

Much of the material on *T.N.T.* (and their subsequent international debut, Atlantic's *High Voltage*) stands head and shoulders above that which appeared on the Australian *High Voltage* debut. In a matter of months the band had already conjured up what would prove to be evergreen and bona fide classics in 'It's A Long Way To The Top (If You Want To Rock 'n' Roll)', 'The Jack', 'High Voltage' and the title track, all staples of AC/DC's scintillating live show over the years.

During these early years the band had lived as a unit in Melbourne, generally regarded as Australia's live music hub; packed off from their native Sydney to earn their spurs, they spent some time in Lansdowne Road in St Kilda and then at the Freeway Gardens Motel in Parkville. Living under one roof helped build a sense of camaraderie; indeed, when Phil Rudd went to Lansdowne Road for his audition, he found the band running around

in their underwear. Such high jinks, coupled with the free-and-easy nature of life as a rock band (even one as hardworking as AC/DC) meant fun and games with the opposite sex came with the territory. In this instance, it extended to sharing not only an address but the women on the scene, and memorably providing the loquacious Bon Scott with the subject for 'The Jack', his ode to shared venereal disease.

Mark Evans, a friend of AC/DC's road manager Steve McGrath, had originally been a guitarist and was working as an accounts clerk when he'd auditioned for the band, while Rudd had performed in several Melbourne bands, including Buster Brown with future Rose Tattoo singer Angry Anderson, and was drumming with Coloured Balls when he auditioned for AC/DC. Their arrival helped define the relentless, thudding backbeat over which the Young brothers would lay down their wall of guitar.

T.N.T. was recorded at Albert Records' studio in Sydney in the summer of 1975. The sound had shifted away from the glam pretensions evident on *High Voltage* and further towards the hard-hitting blues approach. Among the nine tracks is another pointer to the source of the band's inspiration for their driving rock sound: its one cover, Chuck Berry's 'School Days'.

Artistically, *T.N.T.* was head and shoulders above *High Voltage*, and its quality was reflected in much better sales, heralded by two singles, 'High Voltage' (July 1975) and 'It's A Long Way To The Top (If You Want To Rock 'n' Roll)' in December. Both these promotional pushes did much to further the band's cause in their native land. A promotional video for the latter, featuring the band performing on the back of a truck with the Rats Of Tobruk Pipe Band on Melbourne's Swanston Street, proved immensely popular, as did a performance on Australia's national music show *Countdown*, which featured Bon dressed as a schoolgirl in a blonde wig.

It remains the only Australian AC/DC release of which there was no international version on Atlantic Records (though all the tracks eventually appeared on other international releases), but even so, *T.N.T.* did much to set them on their path to glory.

T.N.T.

It's A Long Way To The Top (If You Want To Rock 'n' Roll)/Rock 'n' Roll Singer/The Jack/Live Wire/T.N.T./Rocker/Can I Sit Next To You Girl/High Voltage/School Days

LEFT: A deck of cards produced by Atlantic for 'She's Got The Jack', one of the all-time great AC/DC songs. Produced in classy red, gold and white, the style is more reminiscent of a luxury deck of cards than a promotional gift.

ABOVE: Producer Harry Vanda and Malcolm Young have a chat in Albert Studios during the recording of *Dirty Deeds Done Dirt Cheap*.

RIGHT: AC/DC live in '75. Angus Young rips into another solo as the band rock the park at an open air concert in Sydney.

Bon Scott

"I remember we were in this hotel this one time and we were hanging out in one of the rooms and Bon's got a bit of a party going on. Next thing I know, Bon's run into the room, climbed up on the balcony and jumped off into the swimming pool. It's then I realize we're up on the second floor. I panicked and went running out on the balcony expecting to see Bon lying on the ground, but there he is, in the swimming pool, laughing and joking and with his arm round some girl!"

"Bon was the biggest influence in the band. When he came in it pulled us all together. He had that real stick-it-to-'em attitude." *Malcolm*

That was how AC/DC guitarist Angus Young remembered the band's late, great singer when I interviewed him for *Vox* magazine in 1997, when the *Bonfire* box set was released. As you learn more and more about the enigma that was Bon Scott, the stronger the mental image you get of the man. One thing always rings true; he's the kind of guy you'd have loved to go drinking with.

Bon's tales of wine, women and song are legendary, and they played out perfectly against AC/DC's relentlessly driving, blues-based boogie rock. He could make you laugh at a song about VD, yet make you cry with his lonely tales of the outsider, and always made you chuckle with a nifty double-entendre here, or something blatantly crass there. Without him, AC/DC would never have become the band they are today. With him, it's equally debatable. The saddest thing about Bon Scott's death is that he never got to appreciate the band's development after all the hard work he put in.

He was born Ronald Belford Scott in Kirriemuir, Scotland, on July 9, 1946; parents Charles (Chick) and Isa emigrated to Australia with Bon, brother Graham and sister Valerie in 1952. It's a tale that mirrors to some extent that of the Young family almost a decade later. Four years after arriving in Melbourne the Scotts moved to Perth on Australia's west coast, where young Bon joined the Fremantle Pipe Band as a drummer (later, in his AC/DC days, George Young suggested using bagpipes on the intro to 'It's A Long Way To The Top', wrongly believing that to have been Bon's instrument. Bon duly learnt the bagpipes to play on the song). His bad-boy image with AC/DC was no pose; the young Scott was frequently in trouble with the authorities.

It wasn't long before he was bitten by the rock music bug. He drummed for The Spektors in 1964, and when they became The Valentines he shared lead singer duties with Vince Lovegrove. By 1970, however, he'd tired of the beat sound these bands made and moved to Adelaide, where he fell in with a bunch of hippies by the name of Fraternity. The prog rock band released two albums in Australia before changing their name to Fang and touring the UK, including two fateful gigs with Geordie.

A near-fatal motorbike accident left Bon in a coma; when he eventually recovered, his old mate Vince Lovegrove got him a job driving for AC/DC. The partnership worked; having tired of Dave Evans as their frontman, it wasn't long before Bon had the job. "Anyone that's come to see AC/DC with Dave Evans tonight

ABOVE: Belting out a tune during a concert in Hollywood in 1977. Angus Young's hair is visible in the background.

LEFT: Bon Scott strikes a pose during a photo shoot in Camden, London in August 1979, less than one year before his death.

ain't going to see it because the band have fired him," he announced at his first gig with them; and then he duly got on with the job in hand.

Bon kept on getting on with the job in hand for the next six years, as the tales in these pages attest. He'd probably have kept on doing it in the manner everyone knew and loved, were it not for the fateful night of Monday, February 18, 1980. Bon had been to one of his favourite haunts, The Music Machine in Camden, to see Lonesome No More. After a night drinking whisky with his friend Alistair Kinnear, Scott passed out. Unable to wake him upon returning to his flat in Overhill Road, East Dulwich, Kinnear left the singer in the car to sleep it off. During the night, Scott twisted himself around the gear stick, vomited and choked. When Kinnear was awoken the next morning he asked his visitor to check on the singer and went back to sleep. Not seeing him, the caller assumed Scott had left. When Kinnear woke again that evening he went down to find Scott still in the front seat, not breathing. He was rushed to nearby King's College Hospital: but at 33, Bon Scott was dead.

Scott's personality has continued to loom large over the band. Even on the most recent tour his image appeared on the backdrops, drawing rousing cheers from audiences half of whom probably weren't even born when he died. That's the measure of the influence of the man.

"I've never had a message for anyone in my entire life," he once said, "except maybe to give out my room number."

That was Bon Scott. He was a rock star.

ABOVE: Bon's original handwritten lyrics for 'She's Got Balls'.

RIGHT: Pouring himself a strong one in London, 1976.

Dirty Deeds Done Dirt Cheap

With its slightly sinister titular overtones, inspired partly by Mickey Spillane-style mystery books and in part by the *Beaney and Cecil* cartoons Angus watched as a kid (featuring Dishonest John, who would hand out business cards emblazoned with the words 'Dirty Deeds Done Dirt Cheap'), *Dirty Deeds...* is the first AC/DC album released both on the band's Australian label Albert and on Atlantic Records, their new international home: and yet it perhaps suffers from more anomalies than any of their other LPs.

In keeping with the previous Australian albums, the domestic version features a different sleeve from the one released worldwide on Atlantic. For Australia, it was a bar-room drawing with Angus as a snot-nosed schoolboy flicking a V-sign, with a tattooed Bon lording it over a pool table (the remaining members appeared on the back sleeve), while the Atlantic release (in November 1976, just over a month after the Australian release) had a sleeve by Hipgnosis, whose work had graced such iconic Pink Floyd albums as *The Dark Side Of The Moon* and *Wish You Were Here*, with a typically abstract image based on the loose concept behind the songs on the album: tales from the dark side, featuring a photograph of a group of obvious n'er-do-wells, eyes suspiciously blacked out.

It wasn't just the sleeves that differed. Each version of the LP had a different running order and track listing. It was hard to ignore the disparity between Albert, the Australian label that signed and developed the band in their home country, and Atlantic, with its grander plans for the band. The songs 'R.I.P. (Rock In Peace)', which

RIGHT: Bon caught loud and proud recording *Dirty Deeds...* in Australia in 1976.

BELOW: Rare 45rpm British release EP of 'Dirty Deeds...' The cover illustration mixes classic rock themes with AC/DC's trademark tongue-in-cheek style.

FAR RIGHT: Lovable larrikins biding their time in Australia in 1976.

Dirty Deeds Done Dirt Cheap

(Australian) Dirty Deeds Done Dirt Cheap/Ain't No Fun (Waiting Round To Be A Millionaire)/There's Gonna Be Some Rockin'/Problem Child/Squealer/Big Balls/R.I.P. (Rock In Peace)/Ride On/Jailbreak

(International) Dirty Deeds Done Dirt Cheap/Love At First Feel/Big Balls/Rocker/Problem Child/There's Gonna Be Some Rockin'/Ain't No Fun (Waiting Round To Be A Millionaire)/Ride On/Squealer

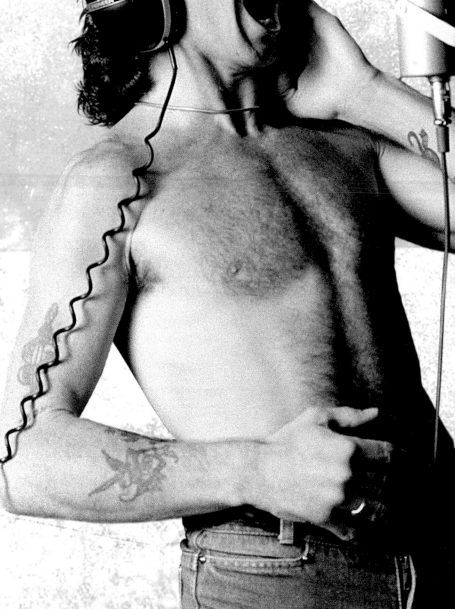

saw Bon honouring rock 'n' roll's famous traditions, and 'Jailbreak', one of the band's most raw and thunderous offerings which was released as a single (backed with the non-album track 'Fling Thing') were left off of the international version of the album, replaced by an edited version of 'Rocker', originally from *T.N.T.*, and 'Love At First Feel', which had only appeared before as the B-side to the single 'Problem Child'; along with 'Cold Hearted Man', on the international version of *Powerage*, it's the only non-album recorded track ever to appear on an AC/DC studio album.

To top it all, adding to the confusion surrounding the release of *Dirty Deeds...*, the album wasn't picked up by Atlantic in America, possibly because it had only released the international version of *High Voltage* in May 1976, possibly because when Atlantic suggested the band decamp to America to further their cause on the world stage AC/DC instead opted to relocate to the UK, which they

felt had more in common with their ideas and ideals. Either way, it might well have taken some of the gloss off the album release.

That in itself is a pity, as the album (either version, if truth be told) rates as a very strong follow-up to the excellent *T.N.T.* (or the international version of *High Voltage*). Although not a concept album per se (AC/DC weren't really ones for such progressively inclined theorizing), the strong narratives injected into the material by lyricist Scott and the relentless driving force provided by the Young brothers (*Dirty Deeds...* is the first AC/DC album featuring exclusively material penned by all three) colour the music perfectly, and in the ominous title track and the rampaging bad-boy anthem 'Problem Child' the band again unleashed what would become AC/DC classics and live favourites.

But *Dirty Deeds...* is not merely a two-song album. 'There's Gonna Be Some Rockin'' and 'Squealer' kick like mules, as does the frenetic

'Rocker', while 'Ain't No Fun (Waiting Round To Be A Millionaire)' is another fine example of Scott's ability to translate events from his own life into a lyrical tale of "them against us" that the band's fans could identify with completely. Best of all, however, were the ribald, tongue-in-cheek 'Big Balls', in which Scott's mastery of the double-entendre came to the fore, and the slow, brooding blues of 'Ride On', which pitched Scott's tale of a loner's life against some brilliant blues soloing from Angus Young.

By the time *Dirty Deeds Done Dirt Cheap* was released AC/DC had already made their first forays out of Australia, relocating to London, where Atlantic housed the band and their crew together in a house in Barnes, replicating their notorious Lock Up Your Daughters tour of Australia on British soil, and drawing favourable reviews from the music press. America would wait for another year, but the rock 'n' roll train was rolling forward with serious momentum.

"We aren't the prettiest things in the world. With AC/DC it's not like we're out to steal your girlfriend and daughter. We may borrow them, but..."

Angus

LEFT: Four of the band and manager Michael Browning toast the band at WEA's London offices. Teetotal Angus drinks milk.

FANTASTIC NEWS!

Cliff Williams

One might imagine, given the nature of a band like AC/DC, that trying out for the Thunder From Down Under would be a pretty traumatic experience. Actually, bassist Cliff Williams sailed through his audition, but there was another hurdle to overcome before he could play a live show with the band he'd just joined: the kind of blinkered bureaucracy AC/DC themselves not only hated, but existed to wind up and overcome. Williams had certainly joined the right band, provided he could get to play with them.

> ## "If something doesn't feel natural to us, we don't do it." *Cliff*

" I had an audition in Pimlico, in a tiny room," recalled the long-haired Williams in 1996. "The first tracks that I played with them were 'Live Wire', 'Problem Child' and, if I can remember, some blues. The manager [Michael Browning] told me afterwards that I had the job. The idea was that I left London to go to Australia to start recording *Powerage*, but the Australian Immigration Service wasn't good with me. In fact, the guy who had my folder told me: 'I don't know why an English musician got the job. An Australian one would have done it fine.' I told him he could have cost me my job."

While the immigration authorities deferred a decision on whether to allow Williams to work AC/DC, who had already recorded a promotional video for the song 'Let There Be Rock' at a church in Sydney's Surrey Hills area, also had two gigs lined up at Bondi Lifesavers Club at which they were hoping to unveil their new bassist. The band got round the irritating officialdom by billing themselves as The Seedies, somewhat obviously, given it was already an Australian nickname for the band. Bondi Lifesavers was overflowing with customers and loud rock 'n' roll on those two nights in July 1977. By the end of the month Williams was with AC/DC for their first tour of America in support of *Let There Be Rock*. Talk about a baptism of fire.

Cliff Williams was born in Romford in Essex on December 14, 1949, although by the time he was 11 the family had moved to Liverpool. At 14, under the spell of The Beatles, The Rolling Stones and The Kinks, he had his own bass guitar, and not long after leaving school decided to try his hand as a professional musician. He moved to London, performing with the likes of the Jason Eddie Rock 'n' Roll Show and the Delroy Williams Soul Show, but wasn't earning very much money and sleeping on floors. Via an ad in music weekly *Melody Maker* Williams met future Wishbone Ash member Laurie Wisefield,

ABOVE LEFT: Attending Rock 'n' Roll Band Camp, at S.I.R. recording studios, Hollywood, California, USA in 2008.

ABOVE: On stage on the first day of the Download Festival in Donington Park, UK on June 11, 2010.

LEFT: Picked out in Camden, London for a photoshoot, 1979. The band was back in the UK.

RIGHT: Crooning on stage at London's Wembley Arena, January 17, 1986.

and the pair formed a band called Sugar. They then formed the progressively minded outfit Home, who managed to secure a deal with Epic Records.

Home released three albums for Epic, but the highlight of their career was playing support to Led Zeppelin at their Electric Magic show at the Empire Pool in Wembley in November 1971. Home also played with Argent, the Faces, Mott The Hoople and The Jeff Beck Group, but when they opted to support Al Stewart in America, their vocalist quit; the band toured as Stewart's own backing band, and Home split on their returning to the UK.

Williams then played with the short-lived Stars before forming Bandit, a more straight-ahead rock band which also featured vocalist Jim Diamond and future Roger Waters drummer Graham Broad. Bandit would eventually act as the backing band for UK blues legend Alexis Korner, although Williams was on the verge of quitting music altogether when the AC/DC call came.

Cliff Williams brings a stoic sense of rhythm to AC/DC as well as a flash of diversity; recording *Powerage*, he was even allowed a small bass solo on 'Sin City'. Williams has played on every album since and at every gig, save for a few dates in 1991 when his place was taken by Paul Greg. He's very much the band's Mr Reliable, and his sense of timing and rhythmic communication with drummer Phil Rudd borders on the psychic.

Now resident in Fort Myers, Florida, with his wife and two children, he's a close neighbour and friend of Brian Johnson, with whom he's performed charity shows for the John Entwistle Foundation. Williams has also performed with Adam Bomb, Emir And The Frozen Camels and local Fort Myers rhythm and blues band The Juice.

But this rhythmic powerhouse has some all too human frailties. Of the leather wrist strap he wears while playing, Williams says: "I protect my right hand because the guitar hurts my fingers. As for the bandage on my arm, it's down to some scarring I've had since I was a child. My skin's fragile there and the bass strap prevents it from getting hurt."

Let There Be Rock

What a difference a year can make. If *T.N.T.* and *Dirty Deeds Done Dirt Cheap* were great albums – and there's been nothing in the ensuing 35-odd years to suggest they're not – then *Let There Be Rock* must surely deserve the title of AC/DC's first classic. The Bon Scott-fronted AC/DC never released a bad album (nor have they since, though some might suggest they lost their way a little in the late 1980s), and they used the first three Australian releases and their relentless touring schedule to fine-tune a barnstorming approach to their craft clearly designed to bring them world domination.

In the period between completing work on *Dirty Deeds...* and the Australian release of *Let There Be Rock* in March 1977 (followed by an international release in June), AC/DC had toured the UK (including both their legendary UK debut at the Brown Cow pub in Hammersmith and their residency at London's Marquee club), returned home to Australia for their Giant Dose Of Rock And Roll tour and supported both Rainbow and Black Sabbath on European jaunts. The latter giving rise to the myth that AC/DC were thrown off the tour after Sabbath bassist Geezer Butler pulled a flick-knife on Malcolm, who retaliated by laying out Butler; in reality Butler had merely been toying with a flick-knife comb, which had annoyed the AC/DC leader, and the final tour dates were in fact cancelled.

Somehow, in between all this, the band found time to return to Albert Studios in Sydney at the start of 1977, again with George Young and Harry Vanda, and in a two-month blast record *Let There Be Rock*, their fourth studio album. AC/DC had learned fast: so when Vanda and Young asked how they wanted their new album to sound, the band demanded they capture their electrifying live sound in the studio.

Comprising a mere eight songs, four per side on the original vinyl, "electrifying" is the perfect word to describe *Let There Be Rock*.

Let There Be Rock

(Australian) Go Down/Dog Eat Dog/Let There Be Rock/Bad Boy Boogie/Overdose/Crabsody In Blue/Hell Ain't A Bad Place To Be/Whole Lotta Rosie

(International) Down/Dog Eat Dog/Let There Be Rock/Bad Boy Boogie/Overdose/Problem Child/Hell Ain't A Bad Place To Be/Whole Lotta Rosie

LEFT: Angus Young rocks America on tour, 1977.

FAR LEFT: An eerily coloured rare version of *LTBR*. A deviation from the regular rock album cover of the time.

LET THERE BE ROCK

"Let there be sound...There was sound/Let there be light...There was light/
Let there be drums...There was drums/Let there be guitar...There was guitar/
Let there be rock!"

"We just want to make the walls cave in and the ceiling collapse. Music is meant to be played as loud as possible, really raw and punchy. And I'll punch out anyone who doesn't like it the way I do." *Bon*

If ever there was a group that could justifiably make biblical pronouncements on the state of rock 'n' roll, AC/DC is *it*. As their debut U.S. release, "HIGH VOLTAGE" (a compilation of their first two Australian LPs), was hitting the streets in the Fall of '76, this Scottish/Australian/English combine was literally tearing up the English/European countryside with their no-holds-barred style. 18-year-old lead guitarist/"schoolboy" Angus Young's onstage outrages helped the group become front page news in many a journal. No less credit is due to the leering aggressiveness of lead singer Bon Scott (30) and compatriots Malcolm Young (24), Phil Rudd (22) and new bassist Cliff Williams (28).

AC/DC started out on New Years Eve 1973 in a little club called Chequers in Sydney, Australia. After several line-up changes, original members/brothers Angus and Malcolm moved to Melbourne and reformed the group with the new additions of Bon, Phil and since-departed bassist Mark Evans. With a sound that was raucous and rocky, they built up a strong initial following on the rough pub circuit throughout 1974 and into early '75. It wasn't long before the club crowds were swollen way beyond normal proportions with the addition of fans who were certainly not a part of the regular pub scene.

After touring steadily for two years "Down Under," AC/DC arrived in the United Kingdom a year ago—virtually an unknown quantity, but it wasn't long before the group had won over the English rock 'n' roll constituency with their high-powered stage act. During a highly successful residency at London's Marquee Club, they kept breaking their own attendance record week after week, getting over 1,000 into a 700-capacity area night after night. Dates all over Europe followed, with equally ecstatic reaction. Having literally taken the Continent by storm, AC/DC returned home in late-1976 for a triumphant 26-date Australian tour.

Adjourning to Sydney's Alberts Studio for January and February this year, accompanied by their famed producing team of Harry Vanda and George Young (Albert Productions), AC/DC put together their fourth album—and second stateside release on ATCO—"LET THERE BE ROCK." Assuredly their most confident effort to date, the song titles alone are quite telling—"DOG EAT DOG," "BAD BOY BOOGIE," "PROBLEM CHILD," "OVERDOSE," "HELL AIN'T A BAD PLACE TO BE..." Coinciding with the LP's release, the boys are embarking on their first-ever assault on U.S. shores. And if the album confirms one's faith in the healthy state of good all-stops-out rock 'n' roll, then be assured that the performances will leave no stone unturned.

ATCO

It's a lean, mean fighting machine of an album full of taut, muscular rock songs that really come close to capturing the magic of AC/DC live. Every band member is on fire as they race through some of their finest songs to date, no mean feat given the plethora of quality material already in their back catalogue.

All the classic AC/DC ingredients are on display: lurid sexual innuendo, paeans to rebellion and tributes to the fans going along for the ride. Of the latter, it's the title track that stands out. This quasi-religious hymn to the power of rock was exactly the kind of thing the band excelled at (and would again with 1981's *For Those About To Rock...*). A promo video, featuring Bon clad in white robes in a pulpit, was shot in a church in Surrey Hills, Sydney, and included the first appearance on film of new bassist Cliff Williams, who would replace Mark Evans following the album's release.

Equally buoyant was the rebel anthem 'Bad Boy Boogie', which when performed live would feature Angus Young's striptease routine; 'Hell Ain't A Bad Place To Be', a catchy tale of life on the road; and 'Dog Eat Dog', a ballsy shot at corporate life. Bon's tales of sexual deviance were never far away, here surfacing on the self-explanatory 'Go Down', while 'Crabsody In Blue' comes on like a sequel to 'The Jack' (indeed, a nervous Atlantic later removed the song from some international versions, replacing it with 'Problem Child' from *Dirty Deeds...*), but the jewel in this particularly opulent crown must surely be album-closer 'Whole Lotta Rosie'. Here Bon's wordplay scales new heights of tongue-in-cheek endeavour, unfolding the tale of a night spent in the company of the titular large lady, which has gone on to become one of the band's best-loved songs and a live favourite. Indeed, it

was voted the number one heavy metal song in the very first issue of *Kerrang!* magazine back in May 1981.

Again, the Australian and international versions of the album were housed in different sleeves: for Australia, a gatefold black and white affair, featuring a blurred shot of fingers on a guitar fretboard (allegedly belonging not to Angus but to Chris Turner, of Aussie prog rockers Buffalo), and for the international version a live shot of the band with Angus caught mid-solo. That cover was also notable for the first use of what became the band's classic logo, created by record company designer Gerard Huerta (who'd also supplied the lightning flashes on the US version of *High Voltage*). With the release of *Let There Be Rock*, everything about this rough-and-ready Australian band was starting to look iconic.

"We've always been a true band. You won't find anyone truer. AC/DC will always be AC/DC." *Malcolm*

Powerage

AC/DC's fifth studio album, released on May 25, 1978, brought with it a string of firsts for the band. It was their first album released more or less simultaneously around the world, and the first released solely on the Atlantic label worldwide. It was the first time the same sleeve was used in all territories and the first AC/DC album to feature new bassist Cliff Williams, previously with UK rockers Home.

Despite these firsts, the album also closed the door on aspects of the band's early career. The arrival of Williams followed Mark Evans' departure; simmering disagreements between the carefree bassist and Angus Young had come to a head after the recording of *Let There Be Rock*. Following the last gig on the European tour supporting Black Sabbath, at Göteborg in Sweden on April 22, 1977, Evans was given his marching orders.

It wasn't just Evans who said goodbye to AC/DC with the advent of *Powerage*. For George Young and Harry Vanda, who had so masterfully developed the AC/DC sound over the band's first four years, *Powerage* was their last AC/DC album until *Blow Up Your Video* in

1988 (Young would return for 2000's *Stiff Upper Lip* album, although by that time he had dissolved his partnership with Vanda). *Powerage* was also the last AC/DC album recorded at Albert's Sydney studio, where they had recorded all their albums to date (although they would continue to use it to record demos). As their international profile grew, so the pressures placed upon the band by their new paymasters began to tell more and more in the wake of *Powerage*.

Perhaps that's one reason why *Powerage*, such a favourite with fans (Rolling Stones guitarist Keith Richards rates it as his top AC/DC album), can sometimes seem overlooked in the band's canon. True, it might not be stacked to the hilt with classics in the same way as

RIGHT: Angus Young atop Bon Scott's steady shoulders at the Oakland Coliseum, California, in 1978.

Powerage

Rock 'n' Roll Damnation/Gimme A Bullet/Down Payment Blues/Gone Shootin'/Riff Raff/Sin City/Up To My Neck In You/What's Next To The Moon/Cold Hearted Man/Kicked In The Teeth

ABOVE: Bon shoots a convivial glance at Angus during a concert in London's Hammersmith Odeon in 1978.

RIGHT: Bon's hairy chest and Angus's bouncing head offer AC/DC's top entertainment, circa 1978.

"I don't think any bastard knows who I am anyway, so I never have any trouble getting mobbed off stage."

Malcolm

Let There Be Rock, but for sheer unbridled ferocity and in capturing the essence of AC/DC's live sound, *Powerage* surpasses all that had gone before it.

Catchy opening track 'Rock 'n' Roll Damnation' is one of the few songs that highlight the band's knack for a melody. It was also the only single off the album, cracking the UK Top 30 for the first time, reaching number 24 in June 1978 and earning the band their first *Top Of The Pops* appearance, and is said to be Eddie Van Halen's favourite AC/DC song. Its equally melodic B-side, 'Sin City', was Bon's disdainful view of the bright lights of Las Vegas, notable for a bass solo for new boy Cliff Williams.

'Riff Raff', one of the album's most powerful songs, swiftly became a live favourite and AC/DC's regular show-opener, the extended intro giving Angus the chance to set the scene with guitar histrionics on a platform above the drum riser before dropping down on to the stage and breaking into his famous duck walk as the band kicked in and the show hit its stride.

The rest of the songs on *Powerage* might not register immediately with the fair-weather fan, but the likes of 'Gimme A Bullet', 'Kicked In The Teeth' and 'What's Next To The Moon' are some of the ballsiest tunes penned during the Bon Scott era. The bluesier refrain of 'Gone Shootin'' allegedly inspired the theme to MTV's cartoon show *Beavis And Butthead* (indeed, it featured in the film *Beavis And Butthead Do America*), and the thrill that ran through the crowd at Milton Keynes Bowl in June 2001 when 'Up To My Neck In You' was reintroduced into the band's set was palpable.

As with every previous AC/DC album, there were one or two track anomalies with *Powerage*. 'Rock 'n' Roll Damnation' had been recorded at the last minute, Atlantic feeling there weren't any potential hit singles on the record. It wasn't finished when the deadline at the pressing plant arrived, so some early copies didn't include it, while other versions were missing the track 'Cold Hearted Man'.

Powerage reached number 26 in the UK album charts, but only a relatively poor 133 in America. Atlantic wasn't happy with the sound of the album, hoping for something more polished that might find favour with FM radio. Maybe that's one reason so many diehard fans enjoy *Powerage* so much: but as the band's next album would show, everything really was about to change.

HIGHWAY TO HELL

AC/DC

SUMMER TOUR
TOWN HALL
CHRISTCHURCH, NEW ZEALAND
★ **ONE CONCERT ONLY** ★
JUNE 30, 1979
8:30 P. M.

LEFT: Poster from New Zealand. This is a bootleg, and has much more of a 1950s feel to it than a 1970s one in terms of fonts used and design.

RIGHT: AC/DC on their best behaviour in a studio photo session in Camden, London in August 1979.

Highway To Hell

There is no doubt *Highway To Hell*, AC/DC's sixth studio album, is the defining moment in their history. True, *Back in Black* would sell far more copies, and is probably the better album. *For Those About To Rock...* gave them their first US number 1, but the strain of maintaining such heady levels of success were beginning to show: and ultimately the shadow of Bon Scott's death would hang heavy over the memory of *Highway To Hell*, as it would over the rest of AC/DC's stellar career, a constant reminder of what might have been, had the fates not dealt the band such a devastating blow.

Like many aspects of the band's career, the story of *Highway To Hell* can be viewed as an us-against-them struggle, the kind AC/DC have always faced head-on, taking their cue from the Youngs' move from Scotland to Australia in 1963. Unhappy with the swaggering *Powerage*, an album it felt was wrong for the US market, Atlantic feared AC/DC's time might already be up if sales didn't pick up considerably. The band had already defied their paymasters by choosing British audiences over American ones in 1976, a move which ultimately paid dividends in cracking the sometimes insular UK market before they headed over to the States in 1977 on the back of *Let There Be Rock*. However, both it and *Powerage* traded on the band's incendiary live sound, lacking the polish and sheen required for acceptance on American FM radio. Though supporting acts of the calibre of Moxy, REO Speedwagon, Rush, UFO and Kiss, they were perhaps too hard-hitting for radio programmers who could dictate public tastes.

It was Atlantic that suggested working not with producers George Young and Harry Vanda, but someone able to make their sound more acceptable to the US market. Given that George was Malcolm and Angus' older brother, their mentor since the band's inception in 1973, the move undoubtedly ruffled feathers within the AC/DC camp, often suspicious of outsiders. Nor should it come as a surprise that the label's original choice didn't last long.

Highway To Hell

Highway To Hell/Girls Got Rhythm/Walk All Over You/ Touch Too Much/Beating Around The Bush/Shot Down In Flames/Get It Hot/If You Want Blood (You Got It)/Love Hungry Man/Night Prowler

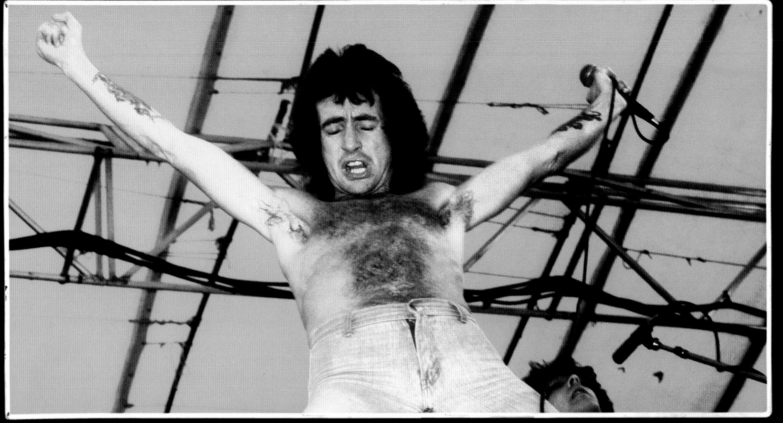

Eddie Kramer had engineered Jimi Hendrix albums in the late 1960s and worked with both Led Zeppelin and Kiss and on paper, at least, looked like someone who could get the required sound out of his new charges. In reality AC/DC were a band who looked to the likes of Chuck Berry, Little Richard and The Rolling Stones for their inspiration (indeed, having supported ZZ Top in America in 1980, AC/DC never opened for another band again until they accepted an offer from the Stones in 2003). Despite working on some demo material back at Albert Studios in Sydney, things didn't gel with Kramer and he was gone within weeks, declaring later: "We did attempt some demos in Australia but I don't think they were that good."

With the pressure on, manager Michael Browning suggested a young South African producer by the name of Robert John Lange, better known as Mutt. His pedigree at that point, confined to working

with New Wave acts such as XTC, The Boomtown Rats and The Motors, didn't seem to suggest the move would succeed; in fact it proved a masterstroke, for all concerned.

Lange instinctively understood AC/DC, their rebellious nature, their goodtime groove, and harnessed their energy. They responded with performances to die for, working in perfect unison with the new producer to create an album that oozed class and finally giving Atlantic a sound they could sell without sacrificing AC/DC's natural swagger.

Apart from the simplistic 'Get It Hot', every track on *Highway To Hell* is a killer, from the taut, seductive riff of the opening title track right down to the ominous closer, 'Night Prowler'. The sound might have been taken up a few radio-friendly notches, but it was still unmistakeably AC/DC: songs about women ('Girls Got Rhythm', 'Beating Around The Bush', 'Touch Too Much'), rebellion ('If You Want Blood...') and life on the road ('Highway To Hell' itself), sounding quite frankly better than AC/DC had ever sounded before.

Highway To Hell was the band's most successful album to date, reaching number 8 in the UK and 17 in America, while the single 'Touch Too Much' again cracked the UK Top 30. Despite drawing attention from the burgeoning Christian right in America for the cover, featuring Angus with devil horns and a tail (in Australia a different cover depicted the band engulfed in hellish flames while a guitar neck suggested a road into the pits of hell itself), and the album's title, and finding themselves embroiled in tabloid hysteria when US serial killer Richard Ramirez was discovered to be a fan of the band and dubbed the Night Prowler, AC/DC were riding high. Little did they know what lay in store.

HIGHWAY TO HELL
EUROPEAN TOUR 79

The 1980s

The 1980s initially started well for AC/DC. Dropping older Young brother George and his Easybeats bandmate Harry Vanda as producers in favour of Mutt Lange had paid dividends, and the resulting album *Highway To Hell* had been their biggest seller yet. The combination of old-style AC/DC grit with a touch of radio-friendly polish had satisfied their paymasters at Atlantic Records, for the time being, anyway, and gone some way towards dispelling the feelings of doubt that might have been creeping into their minds as the relentless touring slog seemed to take its toll. Now the *Highway To Hell* tour was drawing to a close and the future looked bright.

Yet no sooner had the decade begun than they were dealing with tragedy. Bon Scott was discovered dead, aged 33, in a car outside a friend's house in Overhill Road in East Dulwich, South London, after a night of drinking; he had choked on his own vomit. The inquest ruled death was due to acute alcohol addiction and misadventure. It sent AC/DC into a tailspin of grief: yet at Scott's funeral on February 29, his father Chick insisted to Malcolm and Angus that Bon would have wanted the band to carry on without him. By the time the members returned to London, they'd made the decision and the search for a new vocalist had begun. A string of names were mentioned in connection with the band, but in the end 32-year old Brian Johnson, former singer with Geordie, won out.

Back In Black, the band's first album with their new singer and named in Bon's honour, was a monster! Possibly one of the greatest hard rock albums of all time (*the* greatest, if sales figures are to be believed), its reception certainly let the band know that the decision to carry on in the wake of Scott's passing was the right one. The ensuing world tour was also a resounding success, and just over a year after joining the band Johnson found himself back in the studio recording a follow-up.

For Those About To Rock We Salute You was a solid, if unspectacular, sequel, but maintained the band's position at the forefront of the hard rock scene. The ensuing tour, replete with huge cannon going off during the album's title track, was the band's biggest to date and in 1981 they headlined the UK's renowned Monsters of Rock festival for the first time.

However, AC/DC failed to maintain their momentum through the middle years of the decade. Whether this was due to a refusal to heed the changing popular taste in hard rock music or to trouble within the band is a tough one to call given AC/DC's insular nature. Certainly the departure of Phil Rudd during recording of the self-produced *Flick Of The Switch* had an impact, both on the band and on the public's perception of them. Ex-A II Z drummer Simon Wright replaced him and the band headlined Monsters of Rock once more in 1984, but the follow-up album, 1985's *Fly On The Wall*, represented the nadir of the band's recorded output.

Yet in the live arena, AC/DC still managed to thrive. A campaign by America's religious Moral Majority, whose members would picket their shows, had the opposite effect, and the band became even more

popular. They also headlined the inaugural Rock In Rio event in January 1985, playing to audiences of up to a quarter of a million.

In 1986 horror author Stephen King, a massive fan of the band, asked them to contribute the soundtrack for his movie-directing debut *Maximum Overdrive*. The resulting album, *Who Made Who*, gave the band another huge hit with its title track and they once more toured successfully; in 1988 the band were honoured by the Australian recording industry, being inducted in to the ARIA Hall Of Fame.

Who Made Who had reconnected AC/DC with their original production pairing of George Young and Harry Vanda, and the band hooked up with them again for their final album of the decade, *Blow Up Your Video*, which was released in 1988. Although not a particularly strong AC/DC album, it did contain two big hit singles in 'Heatseeker' and 'That's The Way I Wanna Rock 'n' Roll'. The result was the band's biggest-selling album since *For Those About To Rock...* and the ensuing tour was another resounding success.

Despite Malcolm Young requiring time out from some dates on the tour, *Blow Up Your Video* saw AC/DC end the decade as an even bigger band than the one that began it. Certainly in the live arena, there was no one to touch them.

ABOVE: The AC/DC line-up for the bulk of the 1980s, featuring drummer Simon Wright, (right).

LEFT: A classic bootleg album – AC/DC live at the LA forum. This was recorded at their 1982 concert.

Brian Johnson

There's a great story about Brian Johnson's first audition for AC/DC that pretty much captures the measure of the man. Johnson had been cajoled by AC/DC's tour manager Ian Jeffrey into coming down to London to try out for a band whose identity remained a mystery to him. AC/DC had ensconced themselves in North London's E-Zee Hire studios and were working their way through a string of hopefuls.

Initially Malcolm wasn't interested In Johnson; when Mutt Lange suggested the band try the singer out, Malcolm thought he was talking about another member of Geordie. The apocryphal tale of a fan in Chicago suggesting Johnson to the band can be dismissed as myth, although the late Bon Scott had been a fan, having toured with Geordie during his days with Fang, and witnessed what he described as an electrifying show from Johnson, little knowing the singer was suffering from suspected appendicitis on the night.

Both Angus and Malcolm were aware of Geordie, as their Australian label Albert handled the band's publishing and had organized an Australian tour for them, but a confused Malcolm wasn't sold: hence Jeffrey's quiet subterfuge. However, with the band sitting waiting for the new auditionee, Johnson was nowhere to be found. Jeffrey went hunting and eventually discovered the affable Johnson playing pool with the band's crew, whom he'd mistaken for AC/DC themselves, so laid-back and genial was his demeanour. By the time he'd sunk a Newcastle Brown Ale, smoked a tab with the band and sung 'Nutbush City Limits' and 'Whole Lotta Rosie', both Malcolm and Angus knew they didn't need to see any other singers.

Born in Dunston, Gateshead, on October 5, 1947, to an Italian mother and an English father, Johnson discovered both a love of and a talent for music after hearing Johnny Duncan and the Blue Grass Boys on the radio, and developed his voice through involvement with the local choir and appearing in Scout gang shows. Leaving school at 15, he'd studied engineering at technical college and trained as a fitter. His first band were the Gobi Desert Canoe Club and he was spurred on by the successes of local Newcastle bands such as The Animals and a passion for the blues.

After a teenage stint in the army, spending two years in Germany, he returned to join another local band by the name of USA. Within a year they'd changed their name to Geordie and signed a deal with label Red Bus. Geordie began to make some headway with their first single, 'Don't Do That', a kind of glam rock stomper in the mould of Slade. The band would later support Slade and, indeed, had Fang with Bon Scott supporting them at two gigs in Torquay and Plymouth. However, the restrictive deal with Red Bus meant there was never much money and after several reasonable hits, including the Top 10 'All Because of You', and a solo single on EMI, 'I Can't Forget You Now', Johnson had turned his back on music, returning to work as a car roof and windscreen repair man; his brother gave him what would become his trademark cap to keep the glue he used out of his eyes.

He couldn't stay away for long, and was back in another version of Geordie when AC/DC came calling; having landed the gig, Atlantic had to advance him a considerable amount to extract him from the contract he'd signed with Red Bus all those years ago. However, since joining AC/DC Brian Johnson has gone on to become one of rock's best-loved frontmen. In not trying to emulate Bon Scott, for whom he had great admiration, Johnson has allowed his own natural good humour and character to shine through. Rumour says Malcolm originally told Johnson to stand still and shut up between songs, but his naturally garrulous nature and witty comments, still in his broad Geordie accent, are today a major part of the AC/DC show.

Today Brian lives in Sarasota in Florida with his second wife Brenda, an ex-newsreader whom Johnson saw on television and fell for instantly. He has a passion for motor racing; in 2006 he took part in and won the Sky One reality show *The Race* and in 2010 wrote and released *Rockers And Rollers*, an autobiography that centred around his love of automobiles. He currently holds the joint second fastest time in the BBC TV show *Top Gear*'s segment Star In A Reasonably Priced Car.

Outside AC/DC Johnson has worked with the US rock band Jackyl and local Florida band Bad Sara, managed by his wife, and played with AC/DC bassist Cliff Williams on various projects. However, his much-vaunted musical *Helen of Troy*, of which he first spoke in 2003, has yet to see the light of day in its entirety.

RIGHT: "We've got some 'Back In Black' for you now lads…" Brian and Angus milk the applause on the Stiff Upper Lip tour, 2003.

OPPOSITE PAGE: If the cap fits…. Johnson shows off his Northern roots.

PRESS RELEASE ATLANTIC RECORDS PUBLICITY 75 ROCKEFELLER PLAZA, NY 10019 (212) 484-8200

FOR IMMEDIATE RELEASE

FROM: BOB KAUS

APRIL 15, 1980

AC/DC NAMES BRIAN JOHNSON AS NEW LEAD SINGER

Atlantic recording group AC/DC has announced that Brian Johnson has joined the group as their new lead singer. The news comes after the considerable speculation which followed the tragic and untimely death in February of original AC/DC lead singer/lyricist Bon Scott.

27 year-old Brian, who was born just outside Newcastle (England), was previously with the British group Geordie. They enjoyed two Top 20 hits in the U.K. in 1973, "All Because of You" and "Can You Do It." Most recently, Brian had been singing with a re-formed line-up of Geordie, when he was invited to audition for AC/DC last month. Brian was recommended to the group by their producer, Robert John Lange.

Brian has now joined the other members of AC/DC - Angus Young, Malcolm Young, Phil Rudd & Cliff Williams - in rehearsals for the group's next Atlantic album. Current plans call for the band to enter the studio in early May to commence the recording of the new LP.

AC/DC's last album, "HIGHWAY TO HELL," was recently certified platinum by the RIAA. The group most recently toured the U.S. in the Fall of 1979, with a cross-country headlining itinerary.

ATLANTIC RECORDS 9229 SUNSET BLVD. LOS ANGELES, CA 90069

"AC/DC are such a tight family. We've stuck to our guns through the eighties and nineties when people were saying we should change our clothes and style. But we didn't and people got it that we are the real deal." *Brian*

LEFT: The press release that announced Brian Johnson to the world. The style of this plain letter shows its roots in the early 1980s.

OPPOSITE: A pensive looking Johnson gets to grips with his first AC/DC lyrics. Fitting in to the great Bon Scott's shoes was a tall order, but Johnson worked out as a superb addition to the band.

Back In Black

What is there to be said about *Back in Black* that hasn't already been said? An album shrouded in tragedy that became the band's biggest triumph, *Back in Black* has sold close to 50 million copies worldwide, and is the third highest-selling studio album in the history of popular music behind Michael Jackson's *Thriller* and Pink Floyd's *The Dark Side of the Moon* (the latter recently usurping *Back in Black* thanks to a spate of reissues).

And yet the album was recorded under intensely trying circumstances. The band had recently lost much-loved singer Bon Scott on February 19, 1980, found choked to death after vomiting following a heavy drinking session, the inquest verdict was misadventure and acute alcohol poisoning. It was less than a month after the band had concluded their world tour in support of *Highway To Hell*; their final live show with Scott was at Southampton Gaumont on January 27. Bon was cremated on February 29. Only weeks before his untimely death, AC/DC had learned that *Highway To Hell* had sold a million copies in America, a first for the band. On the back of the lengthy tour for the album, some material would undoubtedly have been in progress for what became *Back In Black*: yet its success has always been overshadowed by rumour and conjecture that many of its lyrics were Scott's work. There has never been any evidence that this is the case, although it's widely accepted that the music for 'Let Me Put My Love Into You' and 'Have A Drink On Me' was being developed when Scott died.

Such rumours do a disservice to new frontman Brian Johnson, the ex-Geordie singer who, it was claimed, had won out over a string of higher-profile names such as Steve Marriott, Jimmy Barnes, Allan Fryer and Gary Holton. Having auditioned for the band in early March, he was informed by Malcolm on March 29 that he was AC/DC's new singer. Within a few weeks the band had relocated to Nassau's Compass Point Studios, owned by

Back In Black

Hell's Bells/Shoot To Thrill/What Do You Do For Money Honey/Given The Dog A Bone/ Let Me Put My Love Into You/Back In Black/You Shook Me All Night Long/Have A Drink On Me/Shake A Leg/Rock And Roll Ain't Noise Pollution

Rock And Roll Ain't Noise Pollution
Hells Bells

RIGHT: Angus salutes the crowd. The talented guitarist is capable of performing a full solo with just his left hand – the right pointing to the skies as shown.

BELOW: AC/DC with new singer Brian Johnson outside the rehearsal studios in early 1980.

BELOW, INSET: Blue vinyl release of 'Rock 'n' Roll Ain't Noise Pollution'. It features the same classic contemporary rock sleeve design as the original.

Island Records boss Chris Blackwell, with producer Mutt Lange and engineer Tony Platt, both of whom had worked with AC/DC on *Highway To Hell*.

The new setting was not ideal for swift acclimatization, however. Johnson has gone on record referring to the complex as "breezeblock cells", while being handed fishing spears to repel any Haitian burglars can hardly have been comforting. Having their instruments impounded by customs officials didn't help matters either, while the tropical storm that hit the island soon after their arrival, providing the inspiration for opening track 'Hell's Bells', did little to set the new singer at his ease. However, despite the unfriendly surroundings, and Johnson's own personal discomfort at stepping into a dead man's shoes, the band and crew took him under their wing and he gradually grew into his new role as work on the album continued.

Johnson's vocal performance on *Back In Black* rates as one of his best, hitting such improbably high notes on the likes of the rollicking 'Shake A Leg' that it's rarely been performed live. Lyrically, too, he rose to the occasion, and while not offering the characterful insights fans had come to expect from Scott, he certainly had a similar way with the tongue-in-cheek quip and double-entendre, as evidenced on 'Give The Dog A Bone' and 'You Shook Me All Night Long'.

As for the rest of AC/DC, they played a blinder, driven to new heights by the desire to create an album worthy of their late singer, to whom it was dedicated (the band originally wanted the sleeve to be plain, funereal black; Atlantic forced them to include at least a subtly embossed logo and album title). Each of the ten songs represents the very zenith of creative hard rock songwriting, while the execution of what have become evergreen favourites such as 'Hell's Bells', 'Back In Black' and 'Rock And Roll Ain't Noise Pollution' (the latter giving the band their biggest UK single reaching No. 15) is simply top-notch.

Back In Black would reach number 1 in both the UK and Australia, and hit number 4 in the US. In honouring the tragedy of the band's recent past, AC/DC would also set themselves up for the most phenomenal stage of their career. Little wonder Clinton Walker, author of the excellent *Highway To Hell: The Life Of AC/DC Legend Bon Scott*, called it "the greatest resurrection act in rock history".

For Those About To Rock We Salute You

If ever an album in AC/DC's rich canon of work suggested you could have too much of a good thing, or that even in the cut-throat world of rock music fate can just as easily take away that which she has bestowed upon you, then *For Those About To Rock We Salute You* is that album.

If any other band had come up with the ten songs that make up AC/DC's eighth studio album they'd have been lauded as ground-breaking, but by the time AC/DC convened in Paris in 1981 to begin recording *For Those About To Rock*, they were rapidly being seen as prime movers and shakers in the heavy rock field. Although the band had never liked the "heavy metal" tag pinned to their music – "Heavy metal was always trash," Malcolm once snorted – that particular star had been in the ascendant for the past two or three years, and AC/DC's hard-driving, blues-based rock had merely lifted them towards the top of the new pack of bands who were then usurping the position held throughout the 1970s by the likes of Led Zeppelin and Deep Purple.

Even though they'd worked on a lot of the material for the new album prior to hooking up with Mutt Lange at the Pathé Marconi studios in Paris, the band weren't happy. The decision by Atlantic Records to release *Dirty Deeds...*, their third album, in America some five years after its original release had particularly riled them. Having made such strong inroads into the territory their label rated as the one to break with both *Highway To Hell* and *Back In Black*, it seemed inconceivable that a label should then release an album

with the band's old singer on it. The move, inspired by then-Atlantic president Doug Morris, seemed to be made purely for commercial reasons than anything else.

Equally, AC/DC's arrival in the studio followed rehearsals at apartments in Montmartre which had not gone well. Then there was the problem of Lange. On the one hand, he'd lifted the band's overall sound, adding just the right amount of polish to their rougher edges but allowing the sheer force of the band's natural sound to remain. On the other, his work methods had become increasingly fastidious. It was 1981; his obsession with detail had some way to go before reaching its apotheosis with Def Leppard's 1987 album *Hysteria*, some four years in the making, but Lange's approach was certainly rubbing Malcolm and Angus up the wrong way during the making of *For Those About To Rock....*

Lange was unhappy with the sound he was getting, and the band went through several studios before he put them back in the unpopular Montmartre rehearsal room, this time with the addition of a mobile studio sent from London. The amount of time Lange was taking was particularly annoying Malcolm Young. It didn't help matters when AC/DC's long-booked date at that year's Monsters of

Rock festival at Donington, their biggest UK date yet, appeared on the horizon with progress on the new album still painfully slow.

Though hotly anticipated, not least by the band themselves, AC/DC's headline appearance at Monsters of Rock (the first of a record-breaking three) wasn't a massive success. Within a week the band had fired their management: and Lange, having eventually completed his painstaking work on the new album, would never produce one for them again.

For Those About To Rock We Salute You was both an album and a song that, in the tradition of *Let There Be Rock*, honoured the band, their music and the fans who clamoured to hear it (the title was inspired by Angus' love of history; he had recently read a book about gladiators, who would declare: "Hail, Caesar; we who are about to die salute you" before contests). The sleeve featured an iconic black cannon (in Spain, the original sleeve was black, with a gold cannon), and the big guns came out on the title track too, which would swiftly become the encore for live shows for ever more (although they'd work their way through a series of cannons before getting things right on stage).

Musically it's solid, but lacks the sparkle of *Back In Black*, sounding over-produced in places. 'Let's Get It Up' and the title track were both big UK hits, reaching number 13 and number 15 respectively, while the album hit the top spot in the US and number 3 in the UK: and yet, to date, it's actually sold two million fewer copies than *Dirty Deeds...* has in America. Funny old game, that music business.

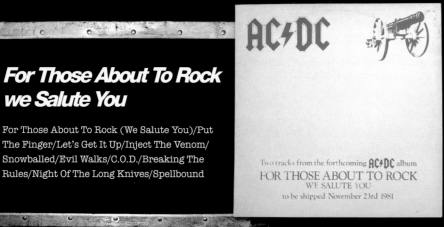

For Those About To Rock we Salute You

For Those About To Rock (We Salute You)/Put The Finger/Let's Get It Up/Inject The Venom/Snowballed/Evil Walks/C.O.D./Breaking The Rules/Night Of The Long Knives/Spellbound

AC/DC

Two tracks from the forthcoming **AC/DC** album
FOR THOSE ABOUT TO ROCK
WE SALUTE YOU
to be shipped November 23rd 1981

OPPOSITE: Brian Johnson, fresh from recording the seminal *Back In Black*, sings his heart out in Toronto in 1981.

LEFT: A rare 12" single promotional only release of 'For Those About To Rock'. The single's cover was reminiscent of the full album cover but done in a minimalist style.

"All the songs we do are about three things: booze, sex or rock 'n' roll."
Bon

ABOVE: Displaying the hair normally hidden under the cap in the UK in 1981.

RIGHT: Visitors pass for *For Those About To Rock* tours.

AC/DC
FOR THOSE ABOUT TO ROCK
AMERICA

VISITORS PASS

DALLAS, TEXAS
FEBRUARY 2, 1982

ABOVE: Dressing room pass for *For Those About To Rock* tours. The design is minimalist and in keeping with the band's branding.

RIGHT: Angus points the way on stage at London's Hammersmith Odeon on the For Those About To Rock tour, 1981.

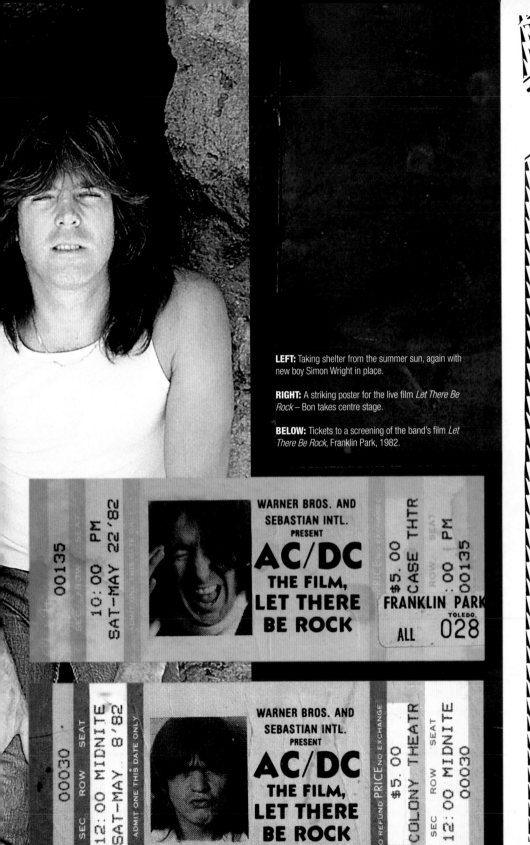

LEFT: Taking shelter from the summer sun, again with new boy Simon Wright in place.

RIGHT: A striking poster for the live film *Let There Be Rock* – Bon takes centre stage.

BELOW: Tickets to a screening of the band's film *Let There Be Rock*, Franklin Park, 1982.

Flick Of The Switch

Self-sufficiency has long been the name of the game with AC/DC and that was never more apparent than with 1983's *Flick Of The Switch*. There's always been a steely determination that's fired the band, one that's undoubtedly born from the upheaval the Young brothers endured in adapting to their new surroundings after their move from Glasgow to Sydney in 1963: from the reaction of conservative Australia of the 1970s to the band's electrifying rock 'n' roll and gleeful embracing of the carefree, full-on life eulogized in the band's lyrics: from facing down similar hostility on their first trips to the UK and America. It is the same inner strength that allowed the band to overcome the tragedy of losing singer Bon Scott: and it was from these deep wells that AC/DC drew strength following 1981's *For Those About To Rock We Salute You.*

"By sticking to what we do, that's being brave." *Brian*

Having rehearsed for four weeks on the Isle of Man, it's notable that the band flew back to Compass Point Studios in Nassau, scene of the creation of their triumphant *Back In Black* album. *Back In Black* engineer Tony Platt was back to help the band out: but it's equally notable that there was no producer, other than Malcolm and Angus themselves, although the final credit for production would be given to the whole band.

Although they certainly had enough studio experience to go it alone, former producer George Young has since admitted that both he and partner Harry Vanda were often on hand to offer advice: but after the rigours of working with the meticulous Mutt Lange on their last three albums, Malcolm had definite ideas about how AC/DC should sound. Muddy Waters' abrasive 1977 album *Hard Again*, which featured a rollicking version of 'Mannish Boy' and was produced by blues guitarist Johnny Winter, was Malcolm's main reference point, while Angus has pointed to the band's desire to recapture their early rawness in the studio.

This they certainly did. *Flick Of The Switch* crackles with abrasive energy. It's interesting that it came out in the same year Def Leppard released the Mutt Lange-produced *Pyromania* and Metallica unleashed their debut *Kill 'Em All*, both giving a clear indication of where hard rock music was headed in 1983. AC/DC's *Flick Of The*

Flick Of The Switch

Rising Power/This House Is On Fire/Flick Of The Switch/Nervous Shakedown/Landslide/Guns For Hire/Deep In The Hole/Bedlam In Belgium/Badlands/Brain Shake

Switch seemed to fall between the two camps.

As such, the album only made it to number 15 in America, but reached number 4 in the UK and Australia. It's regarded as something of a commercial flop, yet it contains some excellent songs, not least 'Nervous Shakedown', 'This House Is On Fire', 'Guns For Hire', 'Bedlam In Belgium' and the awesome title track. All stand up proudly in AC/DC's own extensive body of work.

Again, the recording didn't run smoothly. Problems had been brewing between the hard-headed Malcolm Young and drummer Phil Rudd. Rudd, amiable but quieter by nature than the others, had been hit particularly badly by the death of Bon Scott, retreating into his shell. Matters came to a head midway through recording, developing into a full-blown fist-fight, the exact reason for which has never truly been made clear. What was crystal-clear was that Rudd was out; he left Nassau that day. AC/DC were looking for another new member.

Rudd had by and large completed his drum parts but, strangely, the band asked ex-Procol Harum drummer B.J. Wilson to sit in on sessions for the remainder of the album (although none of his drum parts was ever used). It's said more than 700 people auditioned for the band in America and the UK, including Free/Bad Company stickman Simon Kirke, a particular favourite of Malcolm's, and Roxy Music's Paul Thompson. In the end they went with a little-known Mancunian, Simon Wright, best known as a member of AIIZ and Tytan, both part of the so-called New Wave of British heavy metal, or NWOBHM for short.

With its simple line drawing on the sleeve and its raw intensity, *Flick Of The Switch* was AC/DC sounding as they wanted, having decided *Back In Black* was as 'produced' as they ever wanted to sound. Not everyone shared their vision, however.

LEFT: New drummer Simon Wright gets to grips with his new frontman, Brian Johnson. Both were late additions to AC/DC.

RIGHT: Angus Young holds down a note on the *Flick Of The Switch* world tour, 1983.

ABOVE RIGHT: Drummer BJ Wilson, who was bought in to replace Phil Rudd in the studio while recording *Flick Of The Switch*.

'74 Jailbreak

Jailbreak/You Ain't Got A Hold On Me/Show Business/Soul Stripper/Baby, Please Don't Go

Originally released in North America and Canada in October 1984 (it was released worldwide as part of the band's 2003 reissue programme), this five-track EP allowed the excellent title track a long overdue international release. 'Jailbreak' is taken from 1976's *Dirty Deeds...*, while the other four tracks are all culled from 1975's Australian version of *High Voltage*. Without a doubt, *'74 Jailbreak* was an attempt by Atlantic to cash in on the success of *Dirty Deeds...*, finally released in America in 1981, which had outsold the band's new studio album *For Those About To Rock*.

59

Fly On The Wall

The 1980s were an evolutionary era for heavy rock music. As the decade evolved, so the influence of MTV grew capriciously, thus bringing mainstream media coverage to many of the LA hair metal acts and keyboard heavy melodic rock acts of the era. By the time AC/DC released *Fly On The Wall*, their tenth album, in 1985, the era of hair metal was building towards its zenith, which would come in 1987. To counter the more anodyne mainstream side of metal, the thrash metal movement, pioneered by the likes of Metallica, Megadeth, Slayer and Testament, was also gaining momentum, and indeed would later thrive when leftfield sounds gained further popularity with the advent of grunge.

A t the same time, AC/DC were a phenomenal live draw. Before work began on *Fly On The Wall* the band had headlined at New York's legendary Madison Square Garden, as well as being one of the five headline acts at that year's enormous Rock In Rio festival in January, where they appeared alongside the likes of Yes, Rod Stewart, Ozzy Osbourne and Whitesnake. Their second headline appearance at the UK's Monsters of Rock festival is widely regarded as one of their best, containing the threat of the ascendant Van Halen – tipped by many to blow the headliners away – with consummate ease.

The band had been rehearsing new material for the follow-up to *Flick Of The Switch* before heading to Montreux in Switzerland to begin work on the album proper. Although much of the work was completed at Mountain Studios, then owned by Queen, the backing tracks and vocals were recorded in the very same casino ballroom that hosted the Montreux Jazz Festival, and known to rock fans from Deep Purple's 1971 classic 'Smoke On The Water' (the casino was rebuilt in 1975 after the catastrophic fire which inspired the song).

Once again, and despite some of the problems that occurred with the recording of *Flick Of The Switch*, both Malcolm and Angus helmed the production of *Fly On The Wall*, almost a show of indignation at those detractors who had not welcomed the previous album's rawness. *Fly On The Wall* also witnessed the first studio performance by new drummer Simon Wright, who had replaced Phil Rudd, sacked during the recording of *Flick Of The Switch*. Wright had the whole of the band's previous world tour to bed in, as well

ABOVE: AC/DC seem relaxed enough back in Sydney, Australia (left to right: Cliff Williams, Malcolm Young, Simon Wright, Angus Young, Brian Johnson), but musically the strain of constant recording, touring and promotion was beginning to show – circa 1985.

Fly On The Wall

Fly On The Wall/Shake Your Foundations/First Blood/Danger/Sink The Pink/Playing With Girls/ Stand Up/Hell Or High Water/Back In Business/ Send For The Man

as performing with AC/DC on some of the aforementioned live performances, among the biggest of their career.

The band completed work on the new album (which took its title from a TV advert for fly spray that Angus had seen on television in Australia) in February 1985 and they travelled to Sydney to mix the record. The sessions seem to have run smoothly, despite the odd break for the Rock In Rio shows, although a groundless rumour did

circulate prior to the record's release that Johnson had either left or been fired from the band.

It must be admitted that *Fly On The Wall* does feature one of Johnson's least spectacular performances on an AC/DC album, although his helium-fuelled vocal projections still go some way towards challenging the opposition. However, it wasn't only Johnson who didn't seem to be firing on all cylinders; much of the material seems to fall some way short of the expected AC/DC standard. Indeed, only the ominous groove of 'Shake Your Foundations' and the lyrically lurid 'Sink The Pink' seem to stand out (both featured on the 1986 soundtrack album *Who Made Who*). How many diehard AC/DC fans can actually declare, hand on heart, that they hanker to hear the likes of 'First Blood', 'Back In Business' or 'Send For The Man' every so often?

With both this album and *Flick Of The Switch* AC/DC believed they'd gone some way to recapturing the rough, raw,edgy energy of their early days: but meagre sales of both suggested the sound the band captured for themselves was at odds with what rock fans actually wanted at the time. *Fly On The Wall* only reached number

32 in the US charts. It fared better in the UK, where it made number 7, and back home in Australia the number 4 slot, and in the US there seemed to be an upturn when the band hit the road, and the ensuing tour was a big success.

However, AC/DC's immense popularity did bring with it some drawbacks. It made the band a target for right-wing religious groups who picketed the band's arena shows. Further unwanted headlines came with the arrest of serial killer and AC/DC fan Richard Ramirez, dubbed the Night Stalker, a name uncomfortably close to the band's own title 'Night Prowler': but ultimately the controversy merely added to their appeal, and ticket sales went through the roof.

BELOW: The band, minus drummer Wright, are left propping up the bar in the USA.

"We try to do something with a fresh approach. A lot of people say we work a formula but we don't. We try a fresh approach everytime." *Angus*

LEFT: Brian tolls the famous AC/DC branded 'Hell's Bell' while on tour in the USA in November 1985.

RIGHT: 'Hell's Bells' poster. The song is one of the most popular on *Back In Black*.

Phil Rudd

"The rhythm section is Cliff, Malcolm and myself, and we all lock together to get the groove. We all listen to each other to lock and be tight, because if one person decides to go by himself it doesn't mean anything. We're all looking for the pocket and search for the real feel of the thing, and that's the essence of what we do."

That's how Phil Rudd describes his role in AC/DC's almost mechanical, and most certainly thunderous, rhythm section. It's a fascinating, entirely understandable, insight into the operation of AC/DC's enviable engine room: and yet that Rudd is even a part of the machine today is a remarkable story of triumph over adversity, a story of redemption from what some might perceive as the unlikeliest of sources.

Phil Rudd was born Philip Hugh Norman Witschke Rudcevecuis in Melbourne on May 19, 1954, making him the only native Australian to have held down a long-term position within AC/DC. Rudd caught the drumming bug early, purchasing his own first cheap kit aged 15. His early heroes were the likes of Ringo Starr (he would drum along to The Beatles as a kid), Free's Simon Kirke and The Small Faces' Kenney Jones: anyone, as he put it, who had the ability "to keep time while kicking like a mule." It was an aesthetic that would serve him well.

Rudd played in a variety of local bands: Mad Mole, Charlemagne, Coloured Balls and Krayne, in which his schoolfriend Geordie Leach played bass. He then joined Smack, for whom a certain Gary Anderson would sing. In time Anderson would become known as Angry Anderson and Smack would become Buster Brown. Buster Brown began to make something of a big noise; in November 1974 they appeared before a crowd of 30,000 at the Sunbury Festival. Soon they'd signed to Australian label Mushroom, home to local heroes Skyhooks, for whom they recorded the album Something To Say, which was produced by local guitar hero Lobby Lloyd, However, money was tight, and when Rudd complained about this he was duly given his marching orders.

Meanwhile, current AC/DC drummer Russell Coleman had decided it was time he moved on: and Rudd was washing cars in his father's garage when Coloured Balls drummer Trevor Young (no relation) – who, ironically, had drummed for Buster Brown when Rudd was in Coloured Balls – phoned Rudd to inform him that AC/DC were looking for a new rhythm section. Rudd knew he had no option, and called his mate Geordie Leach asking if he'd accompany him and audition for the vacant bassist role. Leach declined. Rudd, arriving to audition in the hallway of the infamous Lansdowne Road abode, found the band running around in their underwear. He got the gig, impressing Bon Scott – who was a competent drummer himself – with his no-frills attitude.

Rudd's unfussy approach helped define the AC/DC sound. Unjust accusations of crude technique over the years have painted a poor picture of Rudd's skill as a musician: and yet ask any drummer if

ABOVE: Phil Rudd holding down the beat on AC/DC's very first UK tour, 1976. The band played more than 40 gigs in the UK between April and July that year, including in England, Scotland, Wales and the Isle of Man.

they can drum like Phil Rudd and you're likely to be met with a look of astonishment that says: "If only! It's so difficult and yet he makes it look so simple!"

However, it was his attitude that caused his downfall. The quietest, perhaps most inward member of a group of individuals who most certainly didn't opt for the 'group hug' method of man-management, was hit hard by the death of Bon Scott. Already a little too fond of some of the rock 'n' roll lifestyle's excesses, he kept himself more and more to himself. "A little eccentric, nice guy, real angel, a very good heart but very withdrawn," remembered his old partner in the rhythm section, Mark Evans.

As the pressure grew, so a gulf developed between Rudd and Malcolm Young. Matters had come to a head by the end of the *For Those About To Rock* tour. It had evolved into a pressure-cooker situation that had to blow. In the end, it came with a punch-up during the recording of *Flick Of The Switch*.

Rudd was sacked.

The real reason behind the fracas has never been explained by either party, and given AC/DC's nature it's unlikely ever to see the light of day. In any case, it's water under the bridge; amazingly, the notoriously hard-headed Young clan offered Rudd redemption prior to the recording of *Ballbreaker*. He accepted, and he's been the drummer in AC/DC since that day in 1994.

Not that he didn't have other things to keep him busy; he moved to New Zealand in 1983, raising his family and running a farm, a helicopter business and, more recently, a music-themed restaurant: but he craved that second chance. "I didn't want my children to grow up hearing what I'd been," he said. "I thought it would be a good thing if they saw me play while I could."

He got his wish.

ABOVE: Honoured at the Rock Walk hand print ceremony at the Guitar Centre in LA, December 15, 2000.

LEFT: Playing live with AC/DC on tour in Hollywood, California, February 1977.

RIGHT: Phil Rudd strikes a causal pose in a London studio in August of 1979.

Blow Up Your Video

It is a measure of the esteem in which AC/DC are held that they weathered the period after *For Those About To Rock*, which seemingly found them in the creative and commercial doldrums, and ended the decade still one of the most popular bands in their field. They'd begun it coping with the loss of their lead singer, swiftly found a replacement and subsequently recorded what would become not only their greatest album but the third biggest-selling studio album in history.

However, when they began exploring ideas for a new album, initially in Sydney in 1987, their position as one of hard rock's leading lights was under serious threat from the new breed of rock stars such as Bon Jovi, Poison and Guns 'n' Roses, all of whom now hogged the limelight, the airwaves and pages of the world's innumerable new rock magazines.

Despite also having to deal with the loss of long-serving drummer Phil Rudd and declining album sales, the previous two years had seen some positives too. Though 1985's *Fly On The Wall* had been a commercial flop and an ensuing furore had seen US religious zealots picketing AC/DC gigs and claiming the band's name stood for Antichrist Devil Child, their live shows attained more success – no surprise when one considers they have always excelled in the arena.

Malcolm and Angus Young had produced both *Flick Of The Switch* and *Fly On The Wall*, but now the band was reunited with the men known as the Dangerous Dutchman and the Gorgeous Glaswegian, original producers Harry Vanda and George Young, Malcolm and Angus' older brother and mentor. The pair had been an occasional sounding-board during production of the previous two studio albums, but a full reunion came with the song 'Who Made Who', the title track of the band's 1986 soundtrack to the Stephen King movie *Maximum Overdrive*.

The single proved a big success, its radio-friendly sound propelling it to number 16 in the UK singles chart with help from the accompanying video, shot at London's Brixton Academy and featuring hordes of AC/DC fans all dressed as Angus Young. Video producer David Mallet,

who had previously worked with Queen, David Bowie and Rush, would continue to work with the band, who finally seemed to find some comfort with the medium following the poor reception given to the series of promo videos shot for *Fly On The Wall*.

The irony here, of course, is that *Blow Up Your Video*'s title specifically refers to the manner in which rock bands' sound and imagery seemed to pander to MTV, while AC/DC were stating that it'd be better for everyone if they turned their backs on that and went out and saw a live rock band instead: yet the success *Blow Up Your Video* brought them was at least in part down to having embraced this whole side of the media game.

Blow Up Your Video was recorded at the 12th-century Château Miraval in France, where Pink Floyd had recorded *The Wall*. The band had rehearsed at Nomis Studios in London after their Sydney rehearsals, and stuck to a rigid regime, recording from 11am in the morning until 1am. When they headed off to New York to mix the record, they had some 19 tracks to choose from.

Blow Up Your Video would be the most successful AC/DC album since *For Those About To Rock*.... The first single, 'Heatseeker' was a massive success, gaining their highest UK singles chart placing (number 12) and soon becoming a live favourite, while follow-up 'That's

Blow Up Your Video

Heatseeker/That's The Way I Want To Rock 'n' Roll/ Meanstreak/Go Zone/Kissin' Dynamite/Nick Of Time/Sum Sin For Nuthin'/Ruff Stuff/ Two's Up/This Means War

ABOVE LEFT: Angus prepares his striptease routine at Madison Square Garden, New York, USA in 1988.

The Way I Want To Rock 'n' Roll' reached number 22. The reunion with Vanda and Young certainly seemed to have paid dividends.

And yet, is *Blow Up Your Video* a better album than *Flick Of The Switch* or *Fly On The Wall*? In truth, it's not a patch on the former, but scrapes past the latter. The quality of the songwriting is only marginally above that of *Fly On The Wall* and, bar the opening two tracks, the remainder of the album is adequate at best: but it at least recaptured the band's driving sound better than its two predecessors.

The ensuing world tour was also a huge success, even though Malcolm took a leave of absence and was replaced on the tour by his nephew Stevie, son of his older brother Alex (who toured with the band in 1980 as a member of The Starfighters). Thus, while the 1980s may have ended with a touch of uncertainty, AC/DC remained back at the pinnacle of the rockpile: no mean achievement.

LEFT: Brian supplies sturdy shoulders for Angus, live down under in 1988.

RIGHT: Angus in full flow at Birmingham's NEC on the *Blow Up Your Video* tour, 1988.

The Razors Edge

Though generally a troubling decade for AC/DC, the 1980s ended on a high note, the success of *Blow Up Your Video* securing their place at the pinnacle of the rock mountain, although there were still problems to be addressed. The most difficult of these was Malcolm Young bailing on the 1989 *Blow Up Your Video* world tour only a few dates in. Trouble had begun to surface on the *Flick Of The Switch* tour, in the wake of Bon's death and the departure of drummer Phil Rudd. It seemed the stress of being part of one of the world's biggest rock bands was taking its toll.

BELOW LEFT: A rare promotional red vinyl copy of 'Thunderstruck' from the album.

RIGHT: *Razors Edge* backstage pass. The colour choice is a departure from the norm for AC/DC styling.

BELOW: AC/DC dollars, cheekily reproduced to promote 'Moneytalks'. The design style is based on real US dollar bills.

BELOW, BOTTOM: A promotional credit card created for *The Razors Edge*. The shiny gold background and logos give it a look and feel similar to a real card, but the design style is distinctly different and original in font choice to match the rock band's branding.

OPPOSITE: AC/DC with new drummer Chris Slade. Promotional shot, 1990.

alcolm was replaced by his nephew Stevie, son of older brother Alex. Stevie had played guitar in The Starfighters, who had supported AC/DC on the *Back In Black* tour in 1980, and it was said he slotted in so easily most fans who caught the band on the tour wouldn't even have noticed the change. Malcolm would go on to produce Stevie Young's own band, Little Big Horn, in the build-up to recording *The Razors Edge.*

Malcolm's plight wasn't the only potential stumbling-block as AC/DC prepared for their twelfth studio album; drummer Simon Wright had grown restless hanging around between tours, and accepted an offer to work with Dio on their forthcoming album *Lock Up The Wolves*. Malcolm was reported to be unhappy with what he perceived as Wright's staid drumming style, and AC/DC decided it was time to look for another man to sit behind the kit. In the end the job went to Chris Slade, who had previously worked with the likes of Uriah Heep, The Firm and more recently AC/DC's management stablemate Gary Moore.

The final potential troublespot for the band was Brian Johnson. Hitherto, he'd filled the Bon Scott role as lyricist while Malcolm and Angus had provided the musical backdrop, but with work about to start on *The Razors Edge* Johnson was embroiled in a divorce from his first wife and having trouble coming up with new ideas. Malcolm suggested to Angus they step in and help out. It's a role they've

undertaken on the four AC/DC studio albums since.

George Young and Harry Vanda were the band's original choice to produce the new album, on which the band had been working in a barn outside Brighton: but by the time they moved to U2's Windmill Lane Studios in Dublin, it became apparent that George had pressing family matters that needed his attention, and he would not be able to proceed. Eventually, after discussions at Windmill Lane, the name of Bruce Fairbairn entered the frame.

The Canadian producer had been instrumental in developing the career of Canada's melodic rockers Loverboy, as well as masterminding breakthrough albums for Bon Jovi and the re-emergence of US legends Aerosmith: all impressive stuff, but none exactly cut from the same cloth as AC/DC. So Malcolm flew out to Canada to meet Fairbairn, who reportedly impressed the AC/DC leader with the words: "I want you to sound like AC/DC when you were 17." Fairbairn got the nod.

AC/DC went to work on *The Razors Edge* at Fairbairn's Vancouver studios, Little Mountain, and in little more than two months, they were done; things ran so smoothly that the normally undemonstrative Malcolm Young bestowed on Fairbairn a copy of his famous white Gretsch guitar as a token of his appreciation. *The Razors Edge* was released on September 24, 1990.

The album, and ensuing world tour, were massive successes.

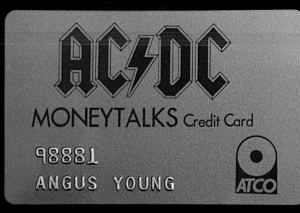

The Razors Edge

Thunderstruck/Fire Your Guns/
Moneytalks/The Razors Edge/Mistress
For Christmas/Rock Your Heart Out/Are
You Ready/Got You By The Balls/Shot Of
Love/Let's Make It/Goodbye and Good
Riddance To Bad Luck/If You Dare

The Razors Edge was the band's biggest-selling album since *For Those About To Rock...*. Opening track and first single 'Thunderstruck' was a natural successor to 'Heatseeker', with its chanting, slow build-up over Angus' frenetic guitar soloing. It immediately became the band's set-opener, and reached number 13 in the UK charts. It was supported by the equally powerful 'Are You Ready', 'Moneytalks' and the epic, Eastern-sounding title track, arguably some of the best songs the band had penned in a long while. Fairbairn's production added just the right amount of modern polish but largely kept the band's trademark power running. If anything, the album was perhaps a track or two over-long, the result of the CD format offering almost 80 minutes of available space for music (more than double the average length of a vinyl album) and both record companies and bands feeling the pressure to fill that up: but, that small grumble aside, *The Razors Edge* took AC/DC back to the very top of their game.

The 1990s

As the decade dawned it was more than apparent that AC/DC had hauled themselves out of any mid-1980s doldrums. If *Flick Of The Switch* hadn't been a bad record, the band's creative flow seemed blocked with *Fly On The Wall*. The song 'Who Made Who' had been a success, and both 'Heatseeker' and 'That's The Way I Wanna Rock 'n' Roll' had maintained the pace, but the remainder of *Blow Up Your Video* hadn't really stood up to close scrutiny.

All that changed at the beginning of the 1990s as the band prepared to release their latest studio album. Although they'd been set to reunite with original producers Vanda and Young, that had ultimately proved impossible due to circumstances beyond anyone's control. Malcolm Young, now firmly back as the band's guiding hand, flew out to meet Canadian producer Bruce Fairbairn. Despite Fairbairn's reputation with melodic rockers such as Bon Jovi and Aerosmith, he impressed Malcolm and the resultant AC/DC album, *The Razors Edge*, fired the band back into the stellar arena to which their reputation entitled them.

The band's biggest-selling album for some time, and the first with new drummer Chris Slade, saw AC/DC as a dominant rock force in the early part of the decade. The accompanying world tour was a massive success, and saw the band headline Donington's Monsters of Rock festival for a record third time, as part of an ongoing European Monsters of Rock tour culminating in a huge show at the Tushino airfield near Moscow, days after the failed military coup which began the dissolution of the old Soviet Union. It was Moscow's first open-air rock concert.

1992 saw the release of *Live*, the band's second live album and the first to feature Brian Johnson. It had been recorded at various gigs from *The Razors Edge* tour, as well as the *Live At Donington* VHS tape, and a year later the band recorded the track 'Big Gun' for the soundtrack to the Arnold Schwarzenegger film *The Last Action Hero*. The song, with its video featuring the Austrian actor dressed as Angus and headbanging with the band, proved to be another big hit.

In 1994 the move was taken that would solidify the band for the remainder of their career to date; Phil Rudd was invited back for rehearsals in the run-up to recording the next album. "He seemed just like the old Phil," stated Malcolm Young, and the *Back In Black* line-up was reunited for *Ballbreaker*, the band's 13th studio album.

For this project the band worked with producer Rick Rubin, and

although Rubin had often declared himself an AC/DC fan, the collaboration had not run smoothly. Fortunately, the album largely succeeded in resurrecting the early AC/DC groove the band had long been searching for, and after which many fans still hankered.

Back out on the road again the band were, incredibly, even more popular than before, The stoic, ballistic beat of Rudd added the drive AC/DC had seemed to lack for much of the 1980s, and their massive new stage show included a giant wrecking ball that had featured on the cover of *Ballbreaker*, on which Brian Johnson would swing and which appeared to demolish half of the immense set.

The band took time out in London to record a small live concert for VH1, the first with Brian and their first live TV exposure since a 1978 US *Midnight Special*. Shot at the station's studios in Camden, the band ran through a selection of material including 'Riff Raff', 'Gone Shootin'' and 'Down Payment Blues', which they'd never played with Brian, and 'Go Down', which they'd never played with Bon either.

At the end of the *Ballbreaker* tour, which would be celebrated with the live video *No Bull*, shot in Madrid in 1997, Angus, Malcolm and elder brother George busied themselves with finally completing their tribute to Bon, some 17 years after his death. A box set entitled *Bonfire* (the name Scott had always said he'd give to his solo album, were he to ever make one) was released. It featured a disc of Scott-era rarities, including an early take on 'Whole Lotta Rosie' entitled 'Dirty Eyes' which was released as a single, plus the unreleased live albums *Live At The Atlantic Studios* and *AC/DC: Let There Be Rock*, as well as a remixed version of *Back In Black*.

The remaining years of the decade were spent working on material for the forthcoming album, although on May 17, 1999, *The Razors Edge* producer Bruce Fairbairn sadly died, aged only 47. Having worked so well with the band at the start of the 1990s to get them back to the top of their game, both Malcolm and Angus attended his funeral. The band were back in Canada within months, working on their next studio album.

PREVIOUS PAGE: The new look AC/DC hit the right notes in London, 1980. (Left to right: Malcolm Young, new singer Brian Johnson, Phil Rudd [hidden] Angus Young, Cliff Williams).

RIGHT: The band taking questions – and finding plenty to laugh about – at a press conference in Sydney Entertainment Centre, with Chris Slade (centre) in October 1991, before their concert there…

OPPOSITE: A still from the record company promotional shot for *The Razors Edge* album, 1990.

Ballbreaker

In the 1990s the game had considerably changed. On the one hand, a band such as AC/DC could tour for at least a couple of years on the back of one album, and these tours would inevitably take in the largest venues in the world. In the wake of the release of 1990's *The Razors Edge*, AC/DC headlined the massive European Monsters of Rock touring festival which also featured the likes of Metallica, Mötley Crüe and The Black Crowes. The event took in a record-breaking third headline appearance at the UK's Donington (a feat never to be repeated, and recorded for prosperity for 1992's *Live* album), as well as headlining before a crowd variously estimated at anything between 100,000 and 2,000,000 when they performed at the Moscow show.

And yet while all this was going on, a vibrant wind of change had swept through the music industry with the advent of grunge music, spearheaded specifically by Nirvana's multi-million-selling *Nevermind* album and the band's anti-corporate rock stance. While no one in their right mind would call AC/DC a corporate rock band, the immense success they garnered would have put them in the firing line of the new wave of grunge-inspired rock fans (ironic, given the immense sales garnered in the early Nineties by the likes of Nirvana, Pearl Jam, Soundgarden and Alice In Chains), even if in the mind of Nirvana's Kurt Cobain the likes of Bon Jovi and Poison were more likely targets. It meant that, having achieved so much on the back of *The Razors Edge*, AC/DC couldn't drop the ball.

However, the big change for AC/DC with *Ballbreaker* was the return of Phil Rudd as drummer. Sacked by the band after an altercation with Malcolm Young during the recording of *Flick Of The Switch*, Rudd had bumped into his old bandmates at a gig in New Zealand on the 1991 tour. That meeting had sown the idea in Malcolm's mind that perhaps Rudd's return might just be the ingredient the band needed to keep ahead of the game. As Angus and Malcolm worked through material for the band's forthcoming new album in London in early 1994, Malcolm called Rudd and asked if he was interested in coming over to drum with the band again. Over he flew, and despite not having drummed for the first six years following his departure, the minute he struck up 'Gone Shootin' and 'What's Next To The Moon', everyone knew the magic was back. AC/DC duly informed Chris Slade his services were no longer required and Phil Rudd was back on board (although no official announcement was ever made of the fact until *Ballbreaker* was released).

Self-proclaimed AC/DC fan Rick Rubin was pencilled in for *Ballbreaker*

Ballbreaker

Hard As A Rock/Cover You In Oil/The Furor/
Boogie Man/The Honey Roll/Burnin' Alive/Hail
Caesar/Love Bomb/Caught With Your Pants Down/
Whiskey On The Rocks/Ballbreaker

ABOVE: Tour programmes and the *Ballbreaker* album box set, featuring the Marvel comic. A classic example of rock art, style and memorabilia.

RIGHT: The Young brothers reunited with drummer Phil Rudd after a break of more than a decade!

after working with the band on the excellent single 'Big Gun' from the 1993 soundtrack to the Arnold Schwarzenegger film *The Last Action Hero*. Rubin's stock as a producer was high; having hit early with the Beastie Boys, he produced The Cult's *Electric* (which one press wag called the best AC/DC album they never made), oversaw the Red Hot Chili Peppers' transformation from alt-rockers to stadium-fillers in their own right, and had worked wonders with the re-emergence of Johnny Cash on the *American Recordings* series of works. The match seemed perfect – at least on paper.

In reality, Rubin and AC/DC didn't work out. His personal eccentricities, such as practising yoga in the studio, didn't go down well with the resolutely working-class AC/DC. He was also working on the Chili Peppers' *One Hot Minute* at the same time as *Ballbreaker*, and his absences from the studio were equally resented. Add in the fact that when he was in the studio Rubin's methodical work practices came

close to the OTT ethic of Mutt Lange, and one can understand the band's disillusionment. When sound issues forced a move from New York's Power Station to Ocean Way in Los Angeles, fears inevitably surfaced that the grim story of *For Those About To Rock...* was about to be repeated. In the end Mike Fraser's credit as co-producer on *Ballbreaker* speaks volumes. As does Malcolm's assertion that Rubin was "not a real rock 'n' roller, that's for sure!"

That said, *Ballbreaker* sounds like a cool AC/DC record. 'Hard As A Rock', 'Hail Caesar', 'Cover You In Oil' and the title track all groove with a *Powerage*-style energy, and the album performed well in the charts, hitting the top spot in Australia, number 4 in the States and number 6 in the UK. The album's title also inspired a new stage set for the ensuing world tour, featuring a giant swinging wrecking ball that would demolish half the set. Along with the success of *Ballbreaker*, the tour kept the band at the top of their game.

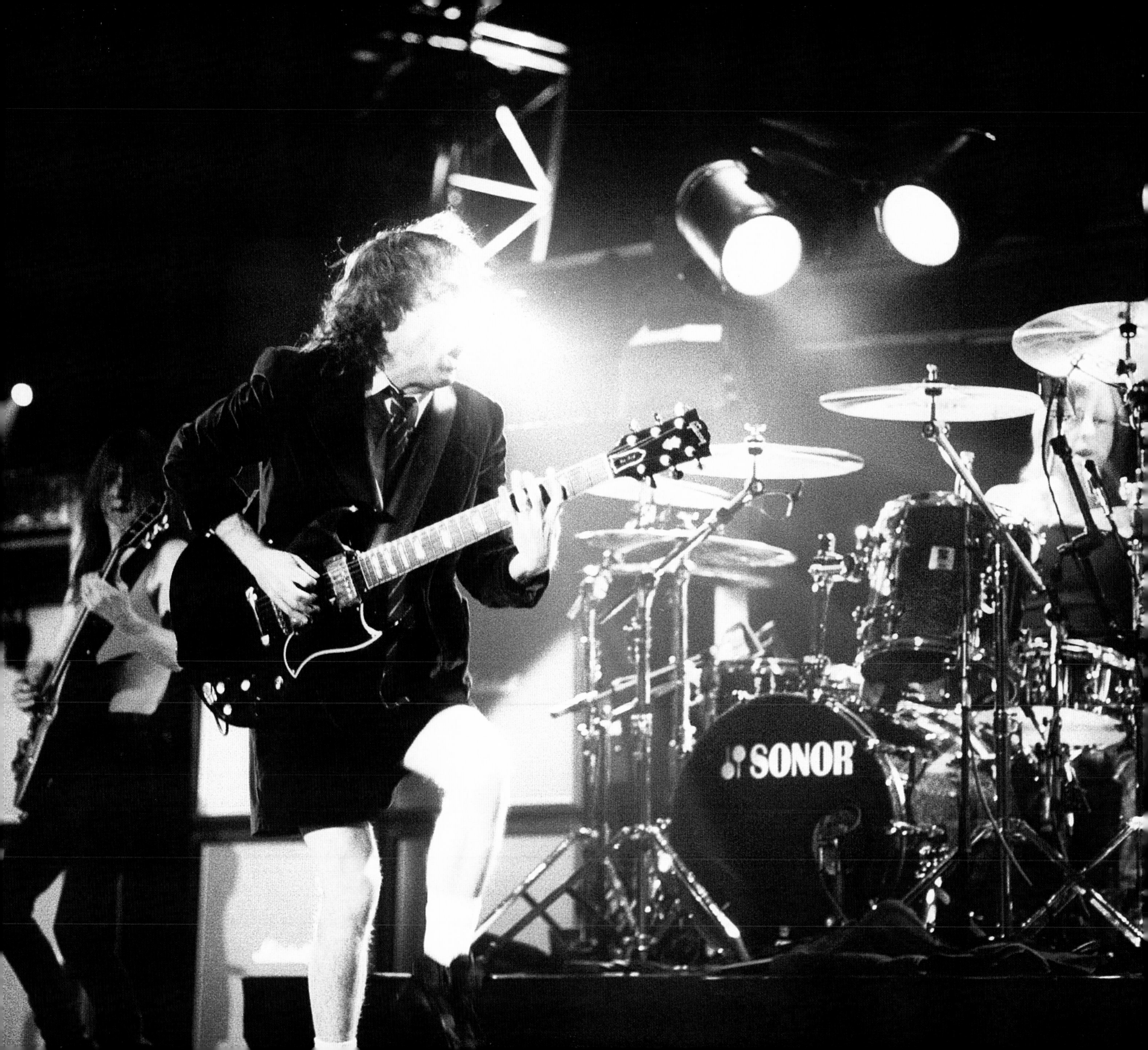
SONOR

Malcolm Young

For a man with a reputation for not saying much, Malcolm Young makes one hell of a big noise, both literally and metaphorically: for despite the "behind-closed-doors" stance AC/DC take with all their business, those who come even remotely close to this amazing rock juggernaut quickly realize that it's Malcolm Young who's in the driving seat.

Until 2014, Malcolm led AC/DC not only on a business level, where his impeccable decisions – no official Best Of albums, new music always being produced – have kept the band at the top for the best part of three decades; his musical drive and vision shaped the very sound of AC/DC from the beginning. Their steadfast refusal to bow to trends and fads; the determination never to take their eye off the ball or forget why the band does what it does; their love of the explosive 1950s rock 'n' roll that changed the face of popular music for ever, combined with a passion for the great bluesmen of America and beyond: and to keep that vision fresh across five decades – well, that's a rare talent indeed.

One perennial rumour, undoubtedly inspired by a photo of Malcolm seated with Angus and elder brother George at a piano, claims their music's successful simplicity comes about because they never record anything unless it can be played on the keyboard. The truth of the matter is that AC/DC begin their songwriting process with acoustic guitars, paring down the essence of the song to its barest yet most effective form before starting the electric guitar process. If it ain't broke you don't fix it, and this approach has served AC/DC better than most. Operating within Malcolm's designated format, each member of the band rises to the occasion time and time again.

Malcolm Young was born on January 6, 1953, in Glasgow, making him a mere two years older than Angus (although early PR for AC/DC suggested Angus was several years his junior). The brothers grew up in the West Sydney suburb of Burwood, attending Ashfield Boys' High School, although neither was a

ABOVE: Malcolm, toting his beloved Gretch guitar, followed by brother Angus, about to take the stage, Australia, 1976.

RIGHT: A youthful Malcolm caught posing during a photo session for *Highway To Hell* in London, 1979.

ABOVE: Malcolm hard at work in the Albert Studio, Sydney in the mid-1970s, probably during the sessions for *Dirty Deeds Done Dirt Cheap*.

RIGHT: Twenty years later, Malcolm was still rocking up a storm, this time on stage in 2001 as part of the *Stiff Upper Lip* tour.

particularly keen student. Both were influenced by music, however, favouring both classic rock 'n' roll, blues and the harder rock sounds of the day, as well as being inspired by their elder brothers Alex, who had formed Grapefruit and was connected to The Beatles, and George, who had hit the big time in Australia with The Easybeats.

Though Malcolm's musical ambitions had little support from his father, who claimed a band featuring him and Angus wouldn't last more than two weeks, hours of practising guitar in his bedroom eventually paid dividends, not just by inspiring Angus but by getting Malcolm into The Velvet Underground, nothing to do with the American band of the same name but a covers band from Newcastle in New South Wales, who specialized in songs by the likes of T-Rex and The Rolling Stones.

Playing other people's songs simply wasn't enough, however, for a young man as driven as Malcolm Young; eventually his desire to form his own band got the better of him and AC/DC was born in 1973. With the support of both older brother George and younger brother Angus, Malcolm's hard-headed desire and drive was key to the band's success. He has, of course, encountered tragedy on the way, when singer Bon Scott died in February 1980 with the band poised on the edge of international stardom. Malcolm felt the need to take time away from AC/DC in 1988, during the band's *Blow Up Your Video* tour. During that time he was replaced by his nephew Stevie who filled in for as long as he was needed. Malcolm was back at the helm to guide AC/DC to even greater commercial success with 1990's *The Razors Edge*. Since then, the band have remained one of the largest draws in rock music, scaling new heights with 2008's massive hit *Black Ice*.

In 2014 the band announced that Malcolm would be taking time away due to ill health, but in September of that year the news was worse: AC/DC's new record *Rock or Bust* would be the first that would not feature Malcolm, and he would not be returning to the band. His place on tour would be taken by nephew Stevie Young instead. Malcolm's musical influence and energy will be missed.

2000s and on...

WA1026 **118** N **12** $0.00 B WA1026
AC/DC
AC/DC
$0.00
B
AC/DC
118
WWW.ACDC.COM
118
N
DOORS AT 6:30PM
N
12
WACHOVIA ARENA
12
WILKES-BARRE, PA
10/21/08
10/21/08
1812669 Sunday, October 26 .00 PM 1812669

555499031103

WACHOVIA ARENA AT CASEY PLAZA

AC/DC released *Stiff Upper Lip*, their 14th studio album, in 2000. A better album than *Ballbreaker*, it nonetheless rankled with some critics who had rarely been able to get the measure of AC/DC since their inception 27 years earlier and accused it of lacking new ideas. These were the critics who frequently criticized the band for making similar-sounding music throughout their career. When informed on the radio show *60 Minutes* that one writer had accused the band of making the same album 12 times, diminutive guitarist Angus laughed: "That's a dirty lie. We've actually made it 14 times."

ABOVE AND RIGHT: Roseland Ballroom ticket, 2003 and Wachovia Arena, 2008. By the 2000s, concert tickets were generic and offered very little in terms of design style as these examples show.

RO0311 FLOOR GA0 113 COMP
EVENT CODE SECTION/AISLE ROW/BOX SEAT
$ 0.00 FLOOR GEN ADM ADMISSION
FLOOR 0.00
ENTRY BY 8PM OR ADMISSION
CA 3X WILL BE DENIED-NO CAMERAS
GA0 113 ROSELAND BALLROOM
DEL601C AC/DC
5MAR03 239 W 52ND ST.,NYC
TUE MAR 11, 2003 8PM

Stiff Upper Lip performed well in some territories, but less well in others. The live tour, however, conforming to most AC/DC tours since 1985's *Fly On The Wall* trek, was another super sell-out. This time, the album sleeve image appeared on stage as a bronzed statue of Angus 40 feet high, snorting smoke and with devil's horns; it was another spectacular visual feast that also found the band once again in particularly fine form.

So popular were AC/DC with the UK's young rock crowd that they headlined three nights at the Milton Keynes Bowl (capacity 65,000), with The Offspring, Queens Of The Stone Age and Megadeth also on the bill.

At the end of the *Stiff Upper Lip* trek, the band took the step of breaking their ties with long-standing label Atlantic. They signed a new deal with the Sony Corporation, with whom their former manager Steve Barnett now held a high management position. The deal included not only the band's extensive back catalogue but new music, leading fans to speculate that a new album would soon be forthcoming. However, it was not to be, sparking further rumours that AC/DC were, in fact, on the verge of calling it a day.

In reality, the band were more than happy for an extensive reissues campaign to be undertaken, easing the pressure as they worked on new material. Cliff had written the music for the film *Chalk*, Phil returned to mess around on his New Zealand farm and Brian, interestingly, announced he had written a musical based on the story of Helen of Troy, a project he conceived with writers Dick Clement, Ian La Frenais and Brendan Healy.

In November 2002 it was announced that AC/DC were to be inducted into the Rock And Roll Hall Of Fame, alongside The Police and The Clash, and in January 2003 Angus and Malcolm appeared on stage in Sydney with The Rolling Stones. The band were duly welcomed into the Hall of Fame in April, by Aerosmith's Steven Tyler with whom they performed 'You Shook Me All Night Long'. Later that year AD/DC played as another band's special guests for the first time since they'd supported ZZ Top back in 1980, when they took a slot with The Rolling Stones for some outdoor shows that culminated in a massive Toronto Rocks event, with Rush also on the bill. Around the same time they played two club shows in Germany and made a special one-off appearance at

their old stamping ground in London, the Hammersmith Apollo, formerly the Odeon, where they hadn't performed for more than 21 years.

Black Ice was released on October 20, 2008, to universal acclaim, charting at number 1 in no fewer than 29 countries. The subsequent world tour was so successful that it ran from October 2008 all the way through to July 2010, including another headline set at Donington, although by this time the event had been renamed the Download festival; AC/DC performed on their own stage.

Post *Black Ice*, the usual rumours did the rounds, fuelled by Brian's suggestion he might retire. Later, he clarified that, at 64, if he felt he couldn't do a live show justice he'd consider retirement,

but anyone who watched the *Live At River Plate* DVD that came out in 2010, or witnessed any of the shows, would have realized Brian Johnson and AC/DC remain as electrifying as ever, and more people than ever seem to want to join the party.

Malcolm Young's temporary, then permanent, withdrawl from the band was sad news for the rock community in 2014 but AC/DC's decision to continue without the founder member was respected and appreciated by fans. The September announcement of the new album *Rock or Bust* whipped fans into a frenzy once more, and the details of a global tour to promote it in 2015 which followed shortly afterwards had the world enthralled. Wherever the journey ends, AC/DC rocked the world!

OPPOSITE: A (by the looks of it enjoyable) photocall from the band's one-off show at Hammersmith Apollo, London, 2003.

RIGHT: Brian Johnson, Angus Young and Malcolm Young, shot for *Rolling Stone* magazine in 2008.

OVERLEAF: AC/DC giving it the *Stiff Upper Lip* on tour in Paris, France, 2003.

Stiff Upper Lip

Considering how recording 1995's *Ballbreaker* with Rick Rubin had stretched the band's patience, it's no surprise that it was all change yet again when AC/DC came to enter the studio towards the end of the 1990s to begin work on their 14th studio album. In the interim they'd worked on the *Bonfire* box set, the band's tribute to late singer Bon Scott which eventually saw the light of day in November 1997 and featured, alongside a remixed version of *Back In Black*, a live soundtrack to the 1979 live movie *Let There Be Rock*, the much-bootlegged *Live At Atlantic Studios 1977* and a disc entitled *Volts* which featured rarities from the Bon era. For this, the band had worked again with Malcolm and Angus' brother George.

In 1999 came the news that Bruce Fairbairn, with whom the band had worked on 1990's *The Razors Edge*, had died suddenly. Malcolm and Angus held him in high esteem for having so effortlessly resurrected the band's career, and both attended Fairbairn's funeral. Upon their return, AC/DC set to work on their latest album, returning to Canada to record in Bryan Adams' Warehouse Studio. Writing of the songs had begun back in 1998 at Angus Young's home in Holland and with Malcolm in London.

Now together in Canada, AC/DC were working with Mike Fraser, a regular Fairbairn associate who had co-produced *Ballbreaker*, and with George Young, who would again be overseeing production, having come out of semi-retirement to help his younger brothers once more.

Once again, as so often throughout the past 20 years when working on a new record, the emphasis for the band was on finding a raw, natural groove, showing they had never lost sight of what made them such a special outfit in the first place. No one would disagree that the majority of their work displayed the essence of what made AC/DC such a uniquely great band (with the possible exceptions of *Fly On The Wall* and *Blow Up Your Video*) but, with Fairbairn on *The Razors Edge*, the combination of Fraser and Young proved ideal for the band on *Stiff Upper Lip*.

The recording sessions went well, and the band left behind 18 new tracks for Mike Fraser to continue mixing in Vancouver, whittling them down to the 12 that would be used on the album. Excluding the band members themselves, few people understood the classic AC/DC sound better than George Young, who has even been described as the band's sixth member, while Mike Fraser is someone who has clearly earned the band's trust and whom they benefit from working with.

Stiff Upper Lip goes further than *Ballbreaker* in an attempt to capture the groove the band were after, and does it far more naturally. When one considers *Ballbreaker* itself was nowhere near being a bad album by any stretch of the imagination, it just shows how good *Stiff Upper Lip* remains: yet, amazingly, it wasn't as successful as its predecessor, only reaching number 12 in the UK, the lowest showing for a chart AC/DC album since *Powerage* in 1978, number 7 in America and number 3 in Australia. It did attain platinum status in America, although *Ballbreaker* has sold twice that amount.

There's a slightly slower groove to the music, with Johnson putting in his most relaxed vocal performance to date. The highlights are clearly the title track, 'House Of Jazz', 'Safe In New York City', the Brian Johnson fave 'Satellite Blues' and 'Can't Stop Rock 'n' Roll'. The sleeve image of a bronze statue of Angus Young once again became

a focal point of the band's latest stage set, breathing fire, growing devil's horns and lighting up at the end of 'Let There Be Rock', while all the inflatables that had appeared over the years, such as the giant Rosie, were all still in evidence.

The tour would run for the best part of a year, from July 2000 to July 2001, with the last leg also including three nights at Milton Keynes Bowl in the unlikely company of The Offspring, Queens Of The Stone Age and Megadeth. A live video, the imaginatively titled *Stiff Upper Lip Live*, was shot at a July gig at Munich's Olympiastadion. In all, *Stiff Upper Lip* and its ensuing world tour were another undoubted success for the band.

ABOVE: Brian and Angus join forces on stage at the Glen Helen Blockbuster Pavilion, Devore, California, USA in 2000.

RIGHT: On stage at the Canadian Rocks for Toronto show in 2003.

LEFT: The band celebrate the Rock Walk hand print ceremony at the Guitar Center in Los Angeles, California, USA in 2000.

Stiff Upper Lip

Stiff Upper Lip/Meltdown/House Of Jazz/Hold Me Back/Safe In New York City/Can't Stand Still/Can't Stop Rock 'n' Roll/Satellite Blues/ Damned/Come And Get It/All Screwed Up/Give It Up

Black Ice

There were eight years between the release of *Stiff Upper Lip* and *Black Ice* seeing the light of day, more than enough time for the AC/DC rumour mill to begin grinding again. Then again, rumours and AC/DC were nothing new and the band's notorious reluctance to respond gave ample fuel to these often incorrect and insidious fires. As far back as the late 1970s rumour was going so far as to suggest Bon Scott might be shown the door prior to *Highway To Hell*. Brian was supposed to have been given the boot before *Fly On The Wall*, and again when his name failed to appear on the songwriting credits for *The Razors Edge*. Prior to *Ballbreaker* word had it that the ensuing world tour would be the band's last and that, heaven forbid, Angus wouldn't even be wearing his trademark school uniform. Indeed, it was much the same when *Stiff Upper Lip* was released. All rubbish, of course.

BELOW: Brian salutes the spotlight in San Antonio, Texas, USA, 2008.

The eight-year wait for *Black Ice* certainly gave the rumour-mongers more than their fair share of material, although there were extenuating circumstances with respect to the delay. Not that AC/DC weren't active in the interim; in 2002 Angus and Malcolm performed with their heroes The Rolling Stones in Sydney and in April 2003 they'd been inducted into the Rock and Roll Hall of Fame, performing 'You Shook Me All Night Long' with Aerosmith's Steven Tyler. The band even accepted an offer to appear as the Stones' special guests at three big outdoor events in Europe, performing two exclusive club dates in Berlin and Munich as warm-ups before a one-off show at London's Hammersmith Apollo (formerly the Odeon), their first there for more than two decades.

In December 2002 AC/DC signed a new deal with Sony Records, where former manager Steve Barnett was now in a senior role, cancelling out their longstanding association with Atlantic. The deal gave Sony the band's back catalogue and also required them to produce new material. However, things were held up by a decision to swap labels within Sony, moving from Epic to Columbia, and when bassist Cliff Williams suffered a hand injury that put him out of action for 18 months the band were more than happy to allow Sony to start reissuing their back catalogue, as it allowed them more breathing space to start work on new material.

In March 2008, however, the band were ready for action once more and headed to Vancouver once again, Angus recalling that he walked into the band's hotel only to see Brian stood at the same bar he'd last seen him at after they'd recorded *Stiff Upper Lip*. Mike Fraser was once again on board as engineer but this time round, at the suggestion of Steve Barnett, Brendan O'Brien was in the producer's chair. O'Brien had previously impressed Malcolm and Angus with his work with the likes of Pearl Jam and Bruce Springsteen. Again the sessions went smoothly, wrapping up in a matter of six weeks after the band had instructed O'Brien to be "brutal".

Black Ice was released on October 17, 2008. It was a colossal success, going straight in at number 1 in an almost unprecedented 29 countries, including the UK, America and Australia, and thus far has sold in the region of six million copies worldwide. Musically, it charts a more rock 'n' roll path than its two predecessors, the band sounding particularly fine on the opening cut 'Rock 'n' Roll Train' (originally intended, as was the album, to be called 'Runaway Train'), 'Big Jack', 'War Machine', 'She Likes Rock 'n' Roll' and the title track, while both the excellent 'Wheels' and 'Anything Goes' actually veer towards pop territory, the first time the band had penned anything so blatantly commercial since 'Moneytalks' from *The Razors Edge*.

Black Ice's success is attributable to a range of factors, perhaps most obviously the quality of the songwriting, the band's performances and the sound O'Brien and Fraser created. It might also be that rock music had become so stale and predictable that the return of a band such as AC/DC on top form came just at the right time. One report suggested that bands like AC/DC thrive by offering escapism at times of economic uncertainty. Whatever the reason, *Black Ice* is one hell of an AC/DC album: perhaps five tracks too long to be an out-and-out classic like *Back In Black*, but still one hell of an AC/DC album, and no mistake.

Black Ice

Rock 'n' Roll Train/Skies On Fire/
Big Jack/Anything Goes/War
Machine/Smash'n'Grab/Spoilin' For
A Fight/Wheels/Decibel/Stormy Day
Monday/She Likes Rock 'n' Roll/
Money Made/Rock 'n' Roll Dream/
Rocking All The Way/Black Ice

ABOVE: Brian Johnson takes the walk of fame in *Black Ice* tour rehearsals, Pennsylvania, USA, 2008…

LEFT: … and Cliff gets to grips with his bass in that same final rehearsal.

FAR LEFT: Big Angus, Little Angus. Either way the guitar playing is electrifying. On stage in 2008.

AC/DC LIVE

LEFT: Angus and Malcolm beneath the giant 'Rosie' inflatable at the Sydney Entertainment Centre.

LEFT: Angus and Malcolm beneath the giant 'Rosie' inflatable at the Sydney Entertainment Centre.

ABOVE: *AC/DC Live* standee. A classically simple piece of minimalist marketing design.

"That hard rhythm is how Malcolm plays and between him, Phil and Cliff, they hold down the back line rhythm and it allows Brian and I to be the colour." *Angus*

Angus Young

He is, of course, one of the most instantly recognizable figures in rock music. At 60, still clad in that trademark schoolboy outfit, cap still perched upon the nodding head, right arm raised in salute, left knee twitching and jerking as he steadily eases himself into the now familiar Chuck Berry-inspired duck walk, Angus Young might confound the pseudo-psychoanalyst critics who find homoerotic significance in an audience of (mostly) middle-aged men paying homage to an even older male, dressed a schoolboy, who will gradually take off more clothes until he bares his bottom to a tumultuous roar. But the packed arenas around the world get it.

"Bon's father grabbed me and Malcolm and said: 'You guys have got to keep going.'" *Angus*

To many, Angus Young is the embodiment of AC/DC, the power behind the Thunder From Down Under: and while that might not be strictly true in purely musical terms he, along first with Bon Scott and now fellow-cap-wearer Brian Johnson, most certainly is the focal point of this most enduring of bands.

Born Angus McKinnon Young in Glasgow, Scotland, on March 31, 1955, Angus was the youngest of the extensive clan born to William and Margaret Young, and was just seven years old when the family emigrated to Australia. He grew up around music, with his three eldest brothers, Steve, John and Alex, entertaining the family with their own homespun band (Alex chose to remain in Scotland when the family moved). Young Angus, much like brother Malcolm, the next eldest, was just as inspired by brother George, who by 1965 had hit the headlines

with The Easybeats, declaring that the appeal lay in seeing his brother's transformation from a 16-year old playing guitar in his bedroom to a pop star being chased down the street by screaming girl fans.

Angus' own forays into music began with an old banjo his mother had given him, to which he added extra strings. Eventually Malcolm passed on his own Hofner guitar to his younger brother; Harry Vanda, George's musical partner in The Easybeats, had handed down his own Gretsch guitar to Malcolm, who developed a lifelong passion for the brand. Eventually Angus himself would progress to the Gibson SG that became his trademark Gibson SG, first with a secondhand 1967 version (today he plays his own signature model).

It wasn't just Angus' male siblings who had an influence on his musical progress. His older sister Margaret was equally influential, taking him to see jazz veteran Louis Armstrong shortly after their

OPPOSITE PAGE, LEFT: Spraying sweat on a stage in 1980 in support of *Back In Black*.

OPPOSITE PAGE, RIGHT: Flailing around on stage on the *Highway To Hell* tour, 1979.

LEFT: Striking a pose in London in April 1976. AC/DC's first London (and UK) concerts were performed that month in England's capital.

RIGHT: A more mature Angus, flanked by brother Malcolm and bassist Cliff Williams, live in Munich, Germany in June 2003 for the *Thunderstruck* tour.

arrival in Sydney, a gig which made an indelible impression on the young Angus. Later she would fashion the various outfits in which Angus would perform as AC/DC found their feet, variously as Super Ang (he would change into his superhero costume in a mock telephone booth on stage, something that swiftly became impractical on Australia's notorious pub circuit stages), Zorro, Spider-Man and even a gorilla. It was at Margaret's suggestion that his old Ashfield Boys' High School uniform was worked into the ultimate schoolboy persona that would become loved the world over. It was also Margaret who noticed the AC/DC letters on the back of her sewing machine and suggested the name might be suitable for the electrifying brand of rock music her brothers' new band traded in.

Having left school, which apart from art classes he rarely enjoyed, as soon as he could (allegedly aged 14 years and nine months), Angus was working as a trainee printer, and saving for his first Gibson SG when he joined his first band, a Sydney group by the name of Kantuckee. They later became Tantrum before Angus, by then 18 years old, joined up with brother Malcolm in the first incarnation of AC/DC.

He's known the world over for his energetic stage antics; the apocryphal tale is that his spasmodic kicking and twirling around on his back (during which, amazingly, Angus maintains his stunning guitar-playing) was born from a desire to duck flying objects at AC/DC's earliest gigs combined with a happy accident at one gig when he fell over his guitar lead but continued playing to make it look like part of the act.

Either way, it all makes him a unique rock talent. His sound is as instantly recognizable as his look, his musicianship such that one can only look on in admiration and wonder how he plays so intricately while maintaining such a wild performance.

Teetotal (the notorious smoker and drinker of tea did once imbibe, when Brian joined the band, which resulted in the band having to put him to bed), Angus lives with his wife in Holland, and Sydney, Australia.

Soundtracks and Live Albums

If You Want Blood You Got It (1978)

AC/DC's first official live album was recorded during the band's *Powerage* tour, on which the band were at their hottest and most ferocious. Although not an entire concert, as was the manner in which live albums were compiled in the 1970s, the bulk of the recordings were made at the band's show at Glasgow's Apollo Theatre on April 30, 1978, and it captures AC/DC in excellent form. The majority of the band's best-known hits at the time feature, including the now-legendary double 'Angus' chant at the beginning of what is deemed the definitive version of 'Whole Lotta Rosie'. The whole concert was filmed and 37 minutes were screened on Scottish TV. Some footage now appears on AC/DC DVD releases but it has never been released in its entirety.

Live (1992)

Not, as widely believed at the time, recorded at the band's record-breaking third headline appearance at Donington Monsters of Rock, although some material was recorded at that show. Other shows on the tour that were recorded for the album were in Moscow, Detroit, Dublin, Glasgow and Edmonton. To date, the only live album to feature Brian Johnson, and recorded because the band felt that by 1991 there was enough Johnson-era material to warrant a live recording. The band were also at a peak of popularity on the back of *The Razors Edge* album. Released initially as a single CD, but a two-disc version and double vinyl album version were released one month later.

Live From The Atlantic Studios (1997)

Although never officially released as a standalone disc, this much sought-after AC/DC collector's item was included in the 1997 box set *Bonfire*. It was originally recorded at Atlantic Records' New York studios to serve as a radio sampler to help promote the band, the first in a series of such recordings Atlantic undertook for their artists. It captures the band in raw form, although only 'Live Wire' and 'Dog Eat Dog' had not surfaced on other live material. Only 5,000 vinyl albums were pressed in 1978 and released to radio stations, although it was transferred to CD in 1986. *Live From The Atlantic Studios* remained one of the most popular AC/DC bootlegs until it was released within the *Bonfire* set, for which it was remixed by George Young.

Let There Be Rock The Movie (1997)

Another live album that was only included in the 1997 *Bonfire* box set tribute to the late Bon Scott. The album is the soundtrack to the film *AC/DC: Let There Be Rock*, which was released theatrically and on VHS back in 1980 and on DVD in June 2011. The recording is taken from an entire concert at the Pavilion de Paris on December 9, 1979, during the band's world tour in support of *Highway To Hell*. The soundtrack differs from the film in that it doesn't contain any of the interviews filmed with the band, while the film doesn't contain the soundtrack version of 'T.N.T.' Both omit the track 'If You Want Blood (You've Got It)', which would have sat between 'T.N.T.' and 'Let There Be Rock' as an encore, although the reasons for this are not known.

OPPOSITE PAGE, ABOVE: Rare, Dutch edition of *If You Want Blood*….
A superb contemporary design for this classic rock album.

OPPOSITE PAGE, BELOW: The thumbs up from the Young brothers at the World
Premiere of the *Live At River Plate* DVD, London, 2011.

ABOVE: The Rock And Roll Train
arrives in Munich…

BELOW: …and in the station at
London's O2 Arena, both 2009.

Who Made Who (1986)

This is the soundtrack to horror author Stephen King's 1986 film
Maximum Overdrive, which was based on the author's short story
'Trucks'. The album is a mix of new material the band recorded specially
and older material from released albums, which at the time made it the
closest thing yet to an AC/DC compilation, something the band had
always adamantly opposed. Aside from the title track, which went on
to be another big hit for the band, they also recorded two instrumental
incidental pieces, 'D.T.' and 'Chase The Ace', which sat alongside the
likes of 'Hell's Bells', 'You Shook Me All Night Long' and sole Bon-era
offering 'Ride On'. Inexplicably, two tracks are featured from *Fly On The
Wall*. Though the film was regarded as a flop, its soundtrack went some
way towards resurrecting the band's career in the mid-1980s.

Iron Man 2 (2010)

Given that only two songs from this album, namely 'Shoot To Thrill'
and 'Highway To Hell', were actually used in the film, while 'Back
In Black' had featured in the original *Iron Man* film, to claim this
15-track album is an actual soundtrack is tenuous, to say the least.
A cynic might be tempted to suggest that the film's connection
to the band was used to get round the policy that AC/DC don't
release compilation albums. Still, with eight tracks from the Brian
era and seven from Bon's, this would have been one very good
AC/DC compilation, if it had officially been one! Released on the
back of the massive success of *Black Ice*, it has sold more than
three million copies and hit the number 1 spot in 11 countries,
including the UK.

Members

Rob Bailey

Bailey played bass with AC/DC between April 1974 and January 1975. He was in the line-up when the band recorded the original *High Voltage*, although George Young actually handled most of the bass parts on the album. Bailey can be seen in the very earliest known clip of the band, performing 'Can I Sit Next To You Girl' at the Last Picture House in Cronulla. Last heard of running a hotel, Bailey has long since left the music business.

Colin Burgess

The original AC/DC drummer joined at the end of 1973 and was fired in February 1974, reportedly for being drunk on stage at Chequers, although he claims his drink was spiked. George Young replaced him for the second set that evening. Now drums with brother Denny in The Burgess Brothers Band.

Ron Carpenter

Replaced Burgess as drummer but lasted a matter of weeks.

Pete Clack

Drummer for the band between April 1974 and January 1975, he was in AC/DC when *High Voltage* was being recorded but it's not known whether he appears on the album.

Russell Coleman

Short-lived AC/DC drummer who replaced Ron Carpenter in February 1974 and was himself replaced by Noel Taylor.

Tony Currenti

Credited as being one of the drummers who appeared on *High Voltage*. Quite possibly just a session drummer.

Dave Evans

The original singer for AC/DC, he fronted the band between November 1973 and September 1974 and sang on the original single 'Can I Sit Next To You Girl'. He was fired when he fell out with the Young brothers, who have since suggested it was down to his glam look; he denied this. He then fronted Rabbit, released two solo albums and appeared in several films.

Mark Evans

Bassist between March 1975 and June 1977. Evans' playing appears on *T.N.T.*, *Dirty Deeds Done Dirt Cheap* and *Let There Be Rock*. He was sacked after falling out with Angus Young. Later played in Heaven and is currently in The Party Boys.

Paul Greg

Mysterious bassist who stood in on the 1991 North American tour when Cliff Williams was absent for reasons unknown.

Bruce Howe

Played bass very briefly for the band in March 1975. Had also appeared in Fraternity with Bon Scott.

Paul Matters

Briefly the band's bassist in March 1975 prior to Mark Evans joining. Appeared in some promo shots around the time. Had previously been in New South Wales band Armageddon.

John Proud

Drummer for AC/DC in November 1974. Had drummed in George Young and Harry Vanda's Marcus Hook Roll Band.

Chris Slade

Shaven-headed drummer for the band following the departure of Simon Wright in 1989. Previously with the likes of Tom Jones, Manfred Mann's Earth Band, Uriah Heep, The Firm and Gary Moore. Appeared on *The Razors Edge* and the subsequent tour. Was ousted when Phil Rudd returned in June 1994. Has since drummed for Asia and Pete Way's Damage Control.

Neil Smith

Bassist for AC/DC between February and April 1974. He replaced original bassist Larry Van Kriedt and in turn was replaced by Rob Bailey. Recently seen in The Swinging Sixties Band.

Noel Taylor

AC/DC drummer between February and April 1974. Currently in 1950s act Legends Of Ol '55.

Larry Van Kriedt

American born musician who was AC/DC's first bass player, and apart from Rudd, the only band member to return to the fold. Kriedt played bass between November 1973 and February 1974 when he was replaced by Neil Smith. He then returned in early 1975 after Rob Bailey had been fired, but was again replaced, this time by George Young. The son of renowned San Francisco jazz musician David Van Kriedt, Larry has since made a name for himself as a jazz saxophonist.

B.J. Wilson

The ex-Procol Harum drummer was much respected by Malcolm Young and drafted in to help out on *Flick Of The Switch* sessions after Phil Rudd had been sacked. None of his parts was eventually used and he was swiftly replaced by Simon Wright.

Simon Wright

Powerhouse Mancunian drummer who replaced Phil Rudd after auditioning for the band in May 1983. Had previous experience with NWOBHM bands AIIZ and Tytan. Wright left AC/DC in November 1989 when he took up an offer to drum on Dio's *Lock Up The Wolves* album. Has since appeared with Dio, AC/DC soundalikes Rhino Bucket and UFO.

Alex Young

Older brother of George, Malcolm and Angus, he stood in on bass for the band in September 1975. Also wrote the song 'I'm A Rebel', reportedly recorded by the band at Albert Studios in 1976 but never released. It was later recorded by German heavy metal band Accept in 1981.

George Young

Older brother of Malcolm and Angus, who operated ostensibly as producer. However, throughout 1974 and 1975 George filled in variously on bass and drum duties as and when required.

Stevie Young

The son of Alex Young and nephew of Malcolm and Angus, he played with AC/DC when Malcolm took time out on the *Blow Up Your Video* tour. Had previously been in The Starfighters, who toured with the band in 1980. Later in Little Big Horn, whose demos were produced by Malcolm. Now retired from the music business.

FAR LEFT: Original singer (1973–74) Dave Evans sinks a drink in 2003.   **LEFT:** Early era bassist Mark Evans backstage in 1976.

BELOW: Chris Slade thumps the tubs.   **BELOW RIGHT:** Simon Wright in 1988.

Discography

Albums

1975
High Voltage (Albert)
T.N.T. (Albert)

1976
High Voltage (Atlantic)
Dirty Deeds Done Dirt Cheap
  (Albert/Atlantic)

1977
Let There Be Rock
(Albert/Atlantic)

1978
Powerage (Atlantic)
If You Want Blood You Got It
  (Atlantic)

1979
Highway To Hell (Atlantic)

1980
Back In Black (Atlantic)

1981
*For Those About To Rock We
  Salute You* (Atlantic)

1983
Flick Of The Switch (Atlantic)

1984
'74 Jailbreak (Atlantic)

1985
Fly On The Wall (Atlantic)

1988
Blow Up Your Video (Atlantic)

1990
The Razors Edge (Atlantic)

1992
Live (Atlantic)

1995
Ballbreaker (Atlantic)

2000
Stiff Upper Lip (Atlantic)

2008
Black Ice (Columbia)

2014
Rock or Bust (Albert/Columbia)

Soundtracks &
Box Sets

1986
Who Made Who (Atlantic)

1997
Bonfire (Atlantic)

2009
Backtracks (Columbia)

2010
Ironman 2 (Columbia)

Singles

1980
'Can I Sit Next To You Girl'

1975
'Love Song'
'High Voltage'

1976
'T.N.T.'
'It's A Long Way To The Top (If
  You Want To Rock 'n' roll)'
'Jailbreak'
'Dirty Deeds Done Dirt Cheap'

1977
'Dog Eat Dog'
'Love At First Feel'
'Let There Be Rock'
'Whole Lotta Rosie'

1978
'Rock 'n' roll Damnation'
'Whole Lotta Rosie' (live)

1979
'Girls Got Rhythm'
'Highway To Hell'

1980
'Touch Too Much'

'Whole Lotta Rosie' (reissue)
'Dirty Deeds Done Dirt Cheap'
  (reissue)
'High Voltage' (reissue)
'It's A Long Way To The Top
  (If You Want To Rock 'n' roll)'
  (reissue)
'You Shook Me All Night Long'
'Hell's Bells'

1981
'Back In Black'
'Big Balls'
'Rock And Roll Ain't Noise
  Pollution'

1982
'Let's Get It Up'
'For Those About To Rock (We
  Salute You)'

1983
'Guns For Hire'
'Nervous Shakedown'
'Flick Of The Switch'

1984
'Jailbreak'

1985
'Danger'
'Sink The Pink'

1986
'Shake Your Foundations'
'Who Made Who'
'You Shook Me All Night Long'
  (reissue)

1988
'Heatseeker'
'That's The Way I Wanna
  Rock 'n' roll'

1990
'Thunderstruck'
'Moneytalks'

1991
'Are You Ready'

1992
'Highway To Hell' (live)

1993
'Dirty Deeds Done Dirt Cheap' (live)
'Big Gun'

1995
'Hard As A Rock'

1996
'Hail Caesar'
'Cover You In Oil'

1997
'Dirty Eyes'

2000
'Stiff Upper Lip'
'Satellite Blues'

2001
'Safe In New York City'

2008
'Rock 'n' roll Train'
'Big Jack'

2009
'Anything Goes'
'Money Made'

2010
'Shoot To Thrill' (live)

Video Albums

1980
AC/DC: Let There Be Rock
  (Warner Bros.)

1985
Fly On The Wall (Atlantic)

1986
Who Made Who (Atlantic)

1989
AC/DC (Albert) Australia only.

1991
Clipped (Atlantic)

1992
Live At Donington (Atlantic)
*For Those About To Rock:
  Monsters In Moscow* (Warner
  Home Video)

1996
No Bull (EastWest)

2001
Stiff Upper Lip Live (Elektra)

2005
Family Jewels (Epic)

2007
Plug Me In (Epic)

2008
No Bull: The Director's Cut
  (Columbia)

2010
Live At River Plate (Columbia)
Let There Be Rock DVD (Warner
  Home Video)

Bon Scott Albums

1971
Fraternity – *Livestock* (Sweet
  Peaches)

1972
Fraternity – *Flaming Galah* (RCA)

1991
*Bon Scott with The Valentines:
  The Early Years* (C5)

1992
*The Legendary Bon Scott
  with The Spektors and The
  Valentines* (See For Miles)

1997
*Bon Scott and Fraternity: The
  Complete Sessions* (Raven)

1998
*Bon Scott: The Early Years
  1967–1972* (See For Miles)

Brian Johnson
Albums

1973
Geordie – *Hope You Like It*
  (Regal Zonophone)

1974
Geordie – *Don't Be Fooled By
  The Name* (Regal Zonophone)

1976
Geordie – *Save The World*
  (Regal Zonophone)

1978
Geordie – *No Good Woman*
  (Red Bus)

1980
Geordie – *Brian Johnson and
  Geordie* (Red Bus)

Cliff Williams
Albums

1971
Home – *Pause For A Hoarse
  Horse* (Epic)

1972
Home – *Home* (CBS)

1973
Home – *Alchemist* (CBS)

1977
Bandit – *Bandit* (Arista)

Phil Rudd Albums

1974
Buster Brown – *Something To
  Say* (Mushroom)

Picture Credits

The publishers would like to thank the following sources for their kind permission to reproduce the pictures in the plate section of this book.

2. Michael Ochs Archives/Getty Images, 4. David Corio/Redferns/Getty Images, 5. Robert Knight Archive/Redferns/Getty Images, 6-11. ©Philip Morris, 14. Bob King/Redferns/Getty Images,15-16. © Philip Morris,17. Michael Ochs Archives/ Getty Images, 18, 20 & 21. © Philip Morris, 22. (left) Fin Costello/Redferns/ Getty Images, 22. (right) Michael Ochs Archives/Getty Images, 23. Dick Barnatt/ Redferns/Getty Images, 24. © Philip Morris, 25. Rex/Chris Capstick, 26-27. Dick Barnatt/Redferns/Getty Images, 28. (left) Neilson Barnard/Getty Images, 28. (right) Neil Lupin/Redferns.Getty Images, 29. (left) Fin Costello/Redferns/Getty Images, 29. (right) Peter Still/Redferns, 30. Ebet Roberts/Redferns/Getty Images, 32. Rex/David Thorpe, 33. Gems/Redferns/Getty Images, 34-35. © Bob Gruen, 36. Richard McCaffrey/Michael Ochs Archive/Getty Images, 37. (left) Rex/Andre Csillag, 37. (right) Chris Walter/WireImage, 38-39. Fin Costello/Redferns/Getty Images, 40. Paul Natkin/WireImage/Getty Images, 41. (top) Richard McCaffrey/ Michael Ochs Archive/Getty Images, 42-43. Rex/Richard Young, 44-45. Deborah Feingold/Corbis, 46. Denis O'Regan/Getty Images, 47. Chris Lopez/Sony Music Archive/Getty Images, 49. & 50-51. Photoshot/Starstock, 51. (right) Michael Ochs Archives/Getty Images, 53. Rex/TB/TS/Keystone USA, 54. Michael Putland/Getty Images, 55. David Corio/Redferns, 56-57. Michael Ochs Archives/ Getty Images, 58. & 59. (centre) Chris Walter/WireImage/Getty Images, 59. (top right) Jan Persson/Redferns/Getty Images, 60. Bob King/Redferns/Getty Images, 61. Ebet Roberts/Redferns/Getty Images, 62-63. Ebet Roberts/Redferns/Getty Images, 63. Bob King/Redferns/Getty Images, 64. Dick Barnatt/Redferns/Getty Images, 65. (bottom left) Michael Ochs Archives/Getty Images, 65. (centre) Newsmakers/Getty Images, 65. (top right) Fin Costello/Redferns/Getty Images, 66. (centre) Ebet Roberts/Redferns/Getty Images, 66. (right) Bob King/Redferns/ Getty Images, 67. Rex/Geoffrey Swaine, 69. Terry O'Neill/Getty Images, 70-71. Michael Putland/Getty Images, 72. Newspix.com, 73. Terry O'Neill/Getty Images, 75. Redferns/Getty Images, 76. (left) Bob King/Redferns/Getty Images, 76 (right) Fin Costello/Redferns/Getty Images, 77. (left) © Philip Morris, 77 (right) Mick Hutson/Redferns/Getty Images, 78. Jo Hale/Getty Images, 79. James Dimmock/ Corbis Outline, 80-81. David Boutard/Kipa/Corbis, 82. (bottom) Newsmakers/ Getty Images, 83. (right) Vaughn Youtz/Getty Images, 83. KMazur/WireImage/ Getty Images, 84. Gary Miller/FilmMagic/Getty Images, 85. (top) Mick Hutson/ Redferns/Getty Images, 85. (bottom) Photoshot/Starstock, 86-87. Bob King/ Redferns/Getty Images, 88. (left) Michael Putland/Getty Images, 88. (right) Rob Verhorst/Redferns/Getty Images, 89. (left) Michael Putland/Getty Images, 89. (right) Stefan M. Prager/Redferns/Getty Images, 90. Jorge Herrera/Getty Images, 91. (top) Stefan M. Prager/Redferns/Getty Images, 91 (bottom) Luke Macgregor/ Reuters/Corbis, 92. (left) Stefan M. Prager/Redferns/Getty Images, 92. (right) Bob King/Redferns/Getty Images, 93. (left) Michael Tullberg/Getty Images, 93. (right) Bob King/Redferns/Getty Images, 94. Rex/Brian Rasic, 95. & 96. Michael Putland/Getty Images

AC/DC memorabilia supplied by Bill Voccia: www.acdccollector.com
Special photography by Cynthia Kirsch Photography: www.kirschphoto.com

Every effort has been made to acknowledge correctly and contact the source and/or copyright holder of each picture and Carlton Books Limited apologises for any unintentional errors or omissions that will be corrected in future editions of this book.

LEFT: AC/DC Lane in Melbourne, Australia.

RIGHT: Brian Johnson – recently made a member of AC/DC – shows off his singing credentials in this concert in London in 1980.